DangerSociety
THE YOUNG BOND DOSSIER

Young Bond isn't afraid of
DANGER – or making ENEMIES.

This dossier takes you right into the heart of Young Bond's
world and includes a never-seen-before EXCLUSIVE Young
Bond story by Charlie Higson, *A Hard Man to Kill*.

Encounter daredevil escapes, deadly weapons and
explore the real-life history featured in the series,
while discovering how to survive the searing heat of
the Mexican desert or an avalanche in the Alps.

Uncover more of James's life at Eton, from the Danger
Society to the Hellebore Cup – plus photos and maps
from all of his adrenalin-fuelled adventures.

No (YOUNG BOND) collection is complete without
this gripping top-secret dossier ...

Before the name became a legend.
Before the boy became the man.
Meet Bond. James Bond.

Books by Charlie Higson

SILVERFIN
BLOOD FEVER
DOUBLE OR DIE
HURRICANE GOLD
BY ROYAL COMMAND

CHARLIE HIGSON

Compiled by A. Li
Illustrated by Kev Walker

PUFFIN

Grateful thanks ... ...ith at Eton College
and John Pulford at the Brooklands Motor Museum

PUFFIN BOOKS

Published by the Penguin Group
Penguin Books Ltd, 80 Strand, London WC2R 0RL, England
Penguin Group (USA) Inc., 375 Hudson Street, New York, New York 10014, USA
Penguin Group (Canada), 90 Eglinton Avenue East, Suite 700, Toronto, Ontario, Canada M4P 2Y3
(a division of Pearson Penguin Canada Inc.)
Penguin Ireland, 25 St Stephen's Green, Dublin 2, Ireland (a division of Penguin Books Ltd)
Penguin Group (Australia), 250 Camberwell Road, Camberwell, Victoria 3124, Australia
(a division of Pearson Australia Group Pty Ltd)
Penguin Books India Pvt Ltd, 11 Community Centre, Panchsheel Park, New Delhi – 110 017, India
Penguin Group (NZ), 67 Apollo Drive, Rosedale, North Shore 0632, New Zealand
(a division of Pearson New Zealand Ltd)
Penguin Books (South Africa) (Pty) Ltd, 24 Sturdee Avenue, Rosebank, Johannesburg 2196,
South Africa

Penguin Books Ltd, Registered Offices: 80 Strand, London WC2R 0RL, England

puffinbooks.com

First published 2009
1

British Library Cataloguing in Publication Data
A CIP catalogue record for this book is available from the British Library

HARDBACK
ISBN: 978–0–141–32768–6

TRADE PAPERBACK
ISBN: 978–0–141–32904–8

CONTENTS

'James Bond was born of a Scottish father, Andrew Bond of Glencoe, and a Swiss mother, Monique Delacroix, from the Canton de Vaud...'

So runs the obituary of Commander James Bond, CMG, RNVR, as printed in *The Times* in 1964. An obituary is a newspaper article that appears when a famous person dies, and which tells you all about them. Of course James Bond wasn't a real person and the obituary appears in *You Only Live Twice*, the eleventh book about Bond, written by his creator, Ian Fleming. In this book M thinks that Bond is dead and writes his obituary. It is the only time in Fleming's books that we find out anything about James's childhood, and it was my starting point when I set out to write about his early years. Fleming goes on to tell us that James's parents died in a climbing accident, and he was brought up by an aunt (Charmian) before being sent off to Eton from where he was expelled because of '*some alleged trouble with one of the boys' maids*'.

From these few scraps of information (by the way – of course James Bond wasn't really dead. He had just gone missing. Bond will never die!), I set out to write five books about Bond at Eton. And what a time we have both had, Bond and I. Just sitting down to write the words 'The name's Bond, James Bond' for the first time sent a tingle down my spine. This wasn't a character *like* Bond, it wasn't his son or a nephew, it was really *him*, the greatest secret agent the world has ever known, and I was writing a story about him. This was quite an honour but also just a little bit scary. If I got it wrong I knew there would be many people out to get me: fanatical Bond nuts, angry children and sinister 00 assassins from MI6. I hope I got it right. So far, at least, I haven't been bumped off.

So what was it like sitting down to write my first James Bond book? In a word – exciting. As a writer you share all your heroes' adventures. So here I was having my own James Bond adventure. Of course he wasn't the adult James Bond. Not yet. I didn't want to write about a super-cool boy in a mini tuxedo with a Walther PPK in his shoulder holster sitting at the wheel of an Aston Martin DB5. That would have been ridiculous. No. It will be a few years before he becomes a secret agent. At the beginning of *SilverFin* James is a fairly ordinary schoolboy, slightly nervous about starting a new school. I wanted to show him growing up over the books and changing from that normal schoolboy into a tougher – and just a little bit sadder – young man, who has seen it all. I wanted to show James losing his innocence and gaining a hard protective shell, so that by the end of book five he would be ready for the adult world. And my hope is that when you, the reader, finish *By Royal Command* you might have some idea why Bond is like he is as a grown-up. A fairly cold-blooded killer. Or should that just be cool?

When I started work on *SilverFin* I already knew how the last book in the series was going to end. Ian Fleming had already told me. It would end with 'some trouble with a boys' maid' and James leaving Eton. I had no idea exactly how I was going to get there but I knew that was where I was heading. Those five books make a set – Bond's Eton years. Of course, there are many more adventures still to come for Bond – there's the rest of his schooldays at a place called Fettes, in Scotland, the outbreak of the Second World War and his initial training with MI6, then his wartime escapades, his earning of the 00 status, and, finally, his early days as a cold war secret agent before he appears in Ian Fleming's original James Bond novel – *Casino Royale*.

I sometimes wonder what Ian Fleming would have made of my books. I don't for one moment think this was the childhood he imagined for his hero. I expect he thought James would have had a pretty normal life before the war broke out. But you lot wouldn't have wanted to read about James doing his homework and playing football and getting a cold and being bored in lessons . . . No. What we want from James Bond is a world of high adventure, so I hope Ian Fleming will forgive me and I do hope he would have liked my stories. I know one thing – he would have been very happy to know just how popular his creation was after all these years. As I said before, Bond will never die and I'm looking forward to all his future adventures.

So what's this new book all about? Well . . . over the course of writing the five Eton stories I've had to find out everything I could about Bond and his world – not just his home life and his school life, but the cars, the guns, the gadgets, the places he visits and the people he meets, as well as what was going on in the world in the 1930s. This dossier is a way of sharing some of that research with those readers who are interested in finding out a bit more about Young Bond's world. The world I have been allowed to play in. But there's more to it than that . . . I couldn't leave Bond behind, and I hope to write many more stores about him in the future, but in the meantime I've written a new one, and filled in a gap – what happened to James on his way back from Mexico after his adventures in *Hurricane Gold* . . .?

To cut a long story short . . . he meets an old friend and makes a new enemy.

All the best,

Charlie

The horse dangled in the air, its legs splayed and waving frantically, its eyes showing white with fear. It whinnied, the sound cutting through all the noises of the dockside. In a few seconds it was twenty, thirty, forty feet in the air as the cargo derrick hoisted it up the side of the ship. The unfortunate beast looked as if it had been grabbed by some giant's hand. Then the crane turned and swung sideways over the deck where it began to slowly lower the horse into the hold until it was out of sight.

Before long the next one would be hoisted up. The girl was already leading it forward to where the stevedores stood waiting. She patted its nose and talked to it. Wouldn't make any difference. Soon the thing would be screaming in terror.

Emil Lefebvre grinned. It was a comical scene. He'd never much liked horses and seeing one in distress amused him. The only thing that would make the spectacle more fun would be if the leather harness broke and one of the big stupid brutes fell to the quayside. He could picture it. The legs galloping in the air, the teeth bared, gasps from the crowd, the girl tearing her hair out, then . . . PAF!

That would be something to see. The horse lying there like a great squashed insect and the girl in tears. Emil chuckled and turned away from the window. Maury and Argente had at last finished their work. The customs inspector had told them all he knew and was now trussed up and gagged. He wouldn't be any more trouble. Emil sighed and mopped his face with a perfumed handkerchief. Why was nothing simple? If the stupid man hadn't been so damned curious, poking around among the packing crates, Emil would be settled on the *Colombie*, sipping a cocktail and casting an appreciative eye over any young ladies who might be on board.

It was a muggy, overcast day. The breeze was from the south, inland, from over the jungles of the interior, so the air in the harbour was thick and damp. He wiped his neck with the handkerchief. Was there no way to stay dry in this godforsaken country?

The customs inspector, a jumped-up peasant with greasy hair, gave a little cry as Maury manhandled him into a chair. They would have to get the poor fellow hidden out of the way somewhere and hope nobody noticed he was missing.

Emil crouched down so that their eyes were on a level. The man's face was raw, puffy and out of shape where Maury and Argente had worked him over. Emil tutted.

'You know, you are looking like you need a holiday, *mon brave*,' he said, smiling. 'A nice long cruise perhaps. The sea air would do you good.'

The man muttered something but the gag muffled his words.

Emil straightened, his knees cracking. He brushed his trousers. They were a pale blue linen and silk mix, shot through with a silver thread that made them shimmer and shine. They were part of a suit, cut specially for him by a tailor in Cuba. He had not dressed for business this morning. If his suit was ruined it would spoil his whole day.

He caught Maury's eye and nodded. Maury drew his knife from the pouch on his belt. Emil was soon bored. He turned to the window again. Another horse was being loaded on to the *Colombie*, its frightened cries masking any sounds the customs officer made. Emil glanced down. There were spots of blood on his burgundy loafers. He swore. They were Italian-made. He bent down to wipe them clean with his handkerchief. Thank God the blood hadn't got on to his clothes. It was nearly impossible keeping smart in this line of work.

And this country. So dirty.

He sighed. He would be very glad to get away from Venezuela.

★

The six-berth pleasure yacht the *Amaryllis* cut through the sparkling blue water of the Caribbean. The only sound, the wind flapping at its sails. A boy sat at the prow: his skin tanned a dark brown, his eyes squinting to keep out the glare of the sun, the spray stinging his cheeks. He was tall and lean and athletic; his body hard, his pale blue eyes slightly cold and distant. His black hair, blowing loose and untidy, hadn't been cut for some time and was crusted with salt.

His name was James Bond.

Ahead, the cluster of small islands that made up the Guadeloupe archipelago were scattered across the sea. The largest of the islands, Basse-Terre, rose up steeply into the sky. It was the tip of a great mountain jutting up from the seabed, its flanks clothed with lush dark-green vegetation. The French name for the mountain La Grande Soufrière, the big sulphur, gave a clue to its origin. It was a volcano, still active.

Behind Basse-Terre was another island, Grande-Terre, separated by a narrow channel known as Salt River. It was there that the *Amaryllis* was heading, to the port of Pointe-à-Pitre.

For a week they had been island-hopping across the Caribbean, from Cuba past Haiti, Puerto Rico and the British Virgin Islands, and now they had reached their final destination: Guadeloupe, the nearest point in the islands to Europe. James had helped to crew the yacht, and the combination of hard physical exertion, sun, sea and swimming had banished the dark clouds from his mind and healed his wounds. Lately his life had been full of violence and fear. He had originally come to this part of the world to recover from injuries he had received in a desperate fight to the death in London. The plan for rest and relaxation, however, had gone horribly wrong when he had got caught up with American gangsters in Mexico. He had left behind some bad memories, but also a handful of good ones. Most of those good memories were to do with a dark-haired girl called Precious Stone. His departure had been bitter-sweet.

He was glad to be putting Mexico behind him and heading for home, but he was sad about leaving the girl. They had shared a wild adventure together and grown very close.

He had saved her life, and she had saved his.

Her grateful father had arranged this little cruise for James and his Aunt Charmian by way of a thank you. The *Amaryllis* was very well equipped for both sport and luxury, and the crew saw to their every need. James and Charmian ate well, most meals featuring seafood straight from the ocean. In the evenings when they put in to port they enjoyed the local nightlife. There would be music and dancing, and in the mornings they would explore the markets. But now they were hurrying under full sail. They had to be in Pointe-à-Pitre this evening to meet the *Colombie*, the French liner that was to take them back to Europe.

The journey across the Atlantic back to Plymouth would be a final chance for James to rest and get his strength back. From there it was going to be another dash to meet up with his friends from Eton who would already be on a skiing trip in the Austrian Alps. Long sea voyages, even on a luxury liner like the *Colombie*, could be dull, but James was looking forward to a stretch of dullness. There was only so much excitement a boy could take before he ended up a gibbering wreck being fed mashed-up food from a spoon.

He had it all planned. He would relax, read some books, play cards and stroll around the deck once a day to get some fresh air and exercise. It would be a leisurely regime of early nights and regular meals.

Yes. He would enjoy being an ordinary boy for a few days.

His Aunt Charmian came along the deck to join him.

'Nearly there,' she said, sitting with her back to the rail. 'There might even be time for a meal in Pointe-à-Pitre if you'd like.'

'I'd be happy to get on board straight away and settle in,' said James.

'I was hoping you were going to say that.' Charmian gave James a relieved smile. 'It's been a busy few days.'

Charmian looked as elegant as always. Despite being an anthropologist and travelling all over the word, often living with very primitive tribes, she always looked smart and unruffled. She kept her hair short and wore simple but well-made clothes. Today, a lightweight summer dress with a large print of tropical flowers and a wide cream sun hat that no matter how windy it was she always somehow managed to keep on her head.

'It will be strange going back to school, I suppose, after all this excitement?' she asked, smoothing down her wind-ruffled dress.

'It's always a wrench,' said James. 'I don't think that school and I are well suited.'

'Don't be in too much of a hurry to join the adult world,' said Charmian. 'You will look back on your schooldays as a time of carefree innocence.'

'Perhaps,' said James, wondering how anything in the rest of his life could compare to the adventures he had already had.

An hour later they were chugging into the harbour at Pointe-à-Pitre, the noise of their diesel engine sounding very loud and intrusive. The *Colombie* was sitting at berth ready to depart, steam rising from her twin red funnels. She was not as large or as fast as the liners that ran the busier New York route, but she was nevertheless an impressive sight. She towered above them, dwarfing the *Amaryllis*, her black hull studded with two rows of portholes, rising to gleaming white upper decks. She was part of the Compagnie Générale Transatlantique fleet, popularly known as the French Line, nearly 488 feet long and able to carry 500 passengers.

As they passed into her shadow James thought how strange it was going to be, moving from the comparatively tiny yacht to the floating hotel that was the *Colombie*.

They moored in a prearranged berth and James and Charmian said their farewells to the captain and crew. The first mate found a porter to take their luggage and they set off along the busy quayside.

Guadeloupe was a French island and although James spoke French fairly fluently he struggled to understand the Creole spoken by the locals, mostly descendents of the slaves who had been brought over from Africa to work on the sugar plantations. James loved the feeling of being somewhere so different to England. He was determined to savour his every brief moment on the island. He was about to leave the Caribbean behind. He had fallen in love with its islands. They had a perfect climate, with warm balmy air, bright skies and refreshing rain bursts. He took it all in: the palm trees, the low colonial buildings, the scents of flowers and spices.

As they neared the gangplanks that serviced the *Colombie* they saw a commotion up ahead and had to stop. Police were keeping a crowd back and there was a great deal of shouting and jostling.

Presently a Black Maria, a reinforced van used for transporting prisoners, arrived at the embarkation point. James struggled to get a view of it through the knot of watching people. The doors of the van opened and two men got out. The driver and his passenger were from the local police, but when they opened the back doors four Europeans emerged and met another white man on the dockside. They all wore the uniform of the French police. There was a short discussion. James could see that the men were tense and alert, nervously looking around at the crowd. They were all smoking heavily. Two carried shotguns.

After another short delay they brought out the prisoner. He had a bag over his head, and his hands and feet were chained. He was short, only a little over five foot, and had a solid square body. James saw that they had removed his shoes.

A murmur went up from the spectators. One word, repeated softy on all sides.

'*Caiboche.*'

Between them the French police led the chained man up the gangplank. He shuffled along awkwardly, yet there was something dignified and unbroken about him, which was accentuated by the nervousness of his captors.

*BETWEEN THEM THE FRENCH POLICE LED THE
CHAINED MAN UP THE GANGPLANK.*

'Is that his name, do you suppose?' James asked Charmian. 'Caiboche?'

'We'll talk about it later,' said Charmian curtly.

Caiboche . . .

The name sounded vaguely familiar but James couldn't place it. Something he had read in a newspaper . . .

He turned to look at Charmian who had a clouded expression on her face.

'Even here in paradise,' she murmured. 'There is wickedness.'

Their cabin was small but comfortable. It consisted of one room with a porthole, two bunk beds, a cupboard, writing desk and chair. There was a small framed print of the ship screwed to the wall.

'I'll take the top bunk,' said James.

'You won't get any argument from me,' said Charmian, undoing the clasp on their trunk, which a porter had brought on ahead.

'You go off and explore if you like,' she said. 'I'll just unpack.'

James left her to it.

The rest of the ship wasn't so cramped. It was done out in the fashionable art deco style; everywhere you looked there were mirrors and cut glass and painted bentwood furniture, with pictures and hangings on every surface. There were several lounges, including a gentlemen's smoking lounge, a dining room with a stage to one side, a bar with polished wood and heavily patterned carpets, a library, a games room, a gymnasium – all of it linked by a maze of corridors and stairways.

As the gangplanks were removed ready for departure James went back to find Charmian so that they could say goodbye to the islands together.

The *Colombie* weighed anchor just as the sun was setting. The passengers lined the railings on the harbour side, and the locals cheered and waved as the great ship moved off at a stately pace, smoke billowing from her funnels and her horns sounding out across the town.

Now there were just four and a half thousand miles of ocean between them and England.

James felt a sharp sting of regret. Soon he would be swapping the brilliant colours and dazzling light of the Caribbean for the flat, dull, grey reality of Britain. At least there was the skiing to look forward to.

He laughed and Charmian asked him why.

'I was thinking about skiing. It's hard to imagine that somewhere in this world there is snow.'

'Ridiculous, isn't it?' said Charmian. 'We've boarded the ship here in the warmth and we shall disembark in chilly Plymouth.'

They stayed at the rail long after the other passengers had drifted away.

'So who is Caiboche?' James asked at last as the sky turned rapidly purple in the startlingly swift Caribbean sunset.

'The butcher of Aziz,' said Charmian quietly, staring at the sea.

'Everybody seems to know who he is except me,' said James.

'Have you heard of the French Foreign Legion?'

'Yes.'

'Do you know why it was set up?'

'No, I'm afraid not. I only know about it from stories like *Beau Geste*.'

'As usual, James, the stories have made a very brutal world romantic and glamorous. The Legion was set up in 1830 after the French decreed that no foreigners were allowed to serve in their regular army. The legion takes men from anywhere, though the officers are all French.'

'Only the officers?' James asked.

'No,' said Charmian. 'They take ordinary Frenchmen as privates. Usually the dregs of society. No questions asked. The Legion was originally set up in the least popular posting of the French colonies, you see. In Algeria in North Africa. And there, in the heat of the desert, the Legion quickly built a reputation for iron discipline and toughness.'

'And this Caiboche was a Legionnaire?'

'Yes. General Charles Caiboche rose from the criminal underworld of Marseilles. A gangster, smuggler, profiteer and murderer, as far as anyone can gather. He escaped capture by joining the Legion. When he was twenty the Great War broke out and the Legion fought with great bravery against the Germans. Caiboche gained a reputation for total fearlessness and utter ruthlessness and in the carnage of that war, where men died in their millions and officers didn't last very long, he quickly rose through the ranks. He survived the battles of Artois and the Somme and after the war returned to Africa. They say he was a good, if strict, officer, and the men were tremendously loyal to him. He was promoted to general, but it seems that was not enough for him. He knew that because of his criminal past he would never be accepted back in France. Maybe the hell of the war destroyed his mind, maybe the desert heat got to him, maybe he was always cracked, but he got delusions of grandeur. He saw himself as a new Napoleon, a new emperor. Something happened out there in Algeria, all those miles from France. Caiboche and half of his men disappeared from the Legion's base. He reappeared some months later in a desert stronghold – an old crusader fort built over a well – at the head of a private army. The ranks had been swelled by Africans, Arabs, Berbers, and criminals from the backstreets of every slum in North Africa, from Casablanca to Cairo. Caiboche declared himself king of the region and promptly set about subduing anyone who disagreed with him. Local Mahdis were assassinated, towns were taken by force. It seems his aim was to take over all of Algeria.'

Charmian fell silent, looking back at the receding lights of Guadeloupe.

'You were in Algeria before I started at Eton, weren't you?' said James.

'I was,' Charmian replied quietly. 'I spent several months in the south with the Tuareg, nomadic Berber tribesmen. I fell in love with the country, its harshness, its savage beauty. I know all too well what Caiboche did out there. At first the French government ignored him, even using him occasionally for their own ends. The locals were always up in arms about something and Caiboche was very good at knocking them back. But in 1928 he set his sights on the fortified town of Aziz, a large and wealthy settlement at the meeting of many important trade routes. I spent a little time there myself when I was travelling in the country. It was a lovely town. I made many friends there.'

'What happened?' James asked.

'The people of Aziz appealed to France for help and a small French force arrived to defend the town. But in a short and violent battle Caiboche overran the defences and sent the French army packing.

'To punish the people of Aziz for standing up to him and "*pour encourager les autres*" – to be a lesson to others – Caiboche slaughtered every man and boy in the city and set up camp there.

'Then the French government finally realized what they were up against and they sent in a much larger force. The second battle of Aziz raged for three days, by which time the town was nothing more than a pile of rubble and Caiboche's army was destroyed.

There was no sign of the general. Those of us who knew about him hoped that he was dead. It appears, though, that he must have escaped across the Atlantic. And now he turns up here in chains. Let us pray that his story is at last over.'

'The French are taking him back to stand trial, I suppose,' said James. 'And they're not taking any chances. Those policemen were armed to the teeth.'

'I do not believe in the death penalty, James,' said Charmian. 'But he is one man I would gladly see hanged.'

The first couple of days on board passed without incident. James took his first wobbly sea steps back towards being a civilized English schoolboy; he had a haircut and got used to wearing shoes and socks and a suit again. He kept to the routine he had imagined on the yacht, and as a result he was soon thoroughly bored. There wasn't enough to do on board to keep him busy. He had tried all the deck games and found them pretty unexciting. He had attended a couple of talks on art and architecture but found his attention wandering. Apart from the crew's quarters, the bridge, the engine rooms and the hold, he had soon explored every inch of the ship. The one little shiver of excitement he got was thinking about General Caiboche. He had quickly discovered where they were keeping him – in one of the first-class suites – and often walked past to see if anything was happening. There were always two of the French policemen sitting outside the door in the corridor, smoking and watching the world go by. James discovered that they were from the Gendarmerie Maritime: the branch of the French security forces that looked after law enforcement at sea.

For the most part the officers kept aloof from the other passengers. They were a tough-looking bunch and stuck together, but there was a young adjutant who was friendlier than the others. He was only a few years older than James and obviously the most junior of the gendarmes. He was forever being sent to run errands for his more senior colleagues. James saw him all the time around the ship and made an effort to get to know him.

His name was René Mathis and he was new to the service. His dream was to join the regular police in Paris, where he was from, but there were more openings in the Gendarmerie Maritime and the opportunity for faster advancement.

'And the faster the better,' he said to James on the morning of the second day as the two of them enjoyed cups of strong French coffee in one of the three cafés on board.

'The other men treat me like their servant, and they are always making fun of me. They call me "*l'enfant*" – the kid. It is tedious for them sitting in there all day watching Caiboche. He never moves. He never speaks. He is like a statue. So they enjoy themselves by playing stupid tricks on me. I cannot wait to get back to France.'

'Did you capture him?' James asked. 'You and the others?'

'*Non.* We are just postmen, making a delivery. We never get to see any excitement.'

'Who caught him, then?'

'The Cuban army.'

'What was he doing in Cuba?'

'When he left Africa he went to South America,' said Mathis, 'where he offered his services to any army who would have him. Nobody wanted him, though. The man was too dangerous. He moved from country to country: Argentina, Bolivia, Brazil, Chile, Mexico – with the same reception wherever he goes – "*Merci, Général*, and *adieu*." It was different in Cuba, however. The army was in charge there; they had decided they could run the country better than the elected government, and Caiboche presented himself to the chief sergeant, a scoundrel named Batista. Batista was looking for a man with no conscience, a man who would kill without thinking. A man like Caiboche. He put him in charge of a secret military murder squad. Anyone who did not like what Batista was up to would one day find Caiboche and his men at their door, and that would be the last anyone ever saw of them. But the French government discover what is going on and ask

Batista kindly if he will give their *général* back to them. Who knows, did Batista want to keep our government happy, or was he worried that Caiboche might become too powerful and threaten his position?' Mathis shrugged. 'But one night Batista invites Caiboche to a cocktail party at the army headquarters. When he arrives Caiboche is arrested and thrown into an army prison cell. Then they sent for us.'

'What's he like?' James asked.

'Caiboche? Pah! Who knows? As I say. He does nothing. He is more of a rock than a man. You would forget he was there except that he stares all the time.' Mathis impersonated him, his eyes wide and glaring. 'For sure he is frightening, so I am happy to stay away and come out here as much as I can.'

On their third night at sea James and Charmian were invited to dine at the captain's table in the lavishly decorated dining room. The food on board was good, the French chefs in the galley saw to that, but James noticed that the food at the top table was just that little bit better. There was caviar, pâté de fois gras and langoustine, lobster, grilled fish, roast rib of beef and a bewildering parade of steamed vegetables.

James sat next to the first officer, Dumas, a big, loud man who made up for the fact that the captain himself was small, elderly and bearded, and said very little. He seemed more interested in his food than in his guests. Dumas took it upon himself to play host and entertain the people round the table with stories and jokes and advice in a slightly heavy-handed manner.

'This wine is not cold enough . . . eight degrees Celsius is the perfect temperature for white wine, or forty-six degrees Fahrenheit as you English would have it . . . Now, we must have more toast . . . the problem is not to get enough caviar, but to get enough toast to go with it, *non*? Am I not right? Ha!'

On James's other side was a thin Brazilian woman with leathery skin that was dried out from being too long in the sun. She was an aristocrat of some sort, weighed down with jewellery. Her lips were a great red stripe of lipstick and her purple eye shadow looked like it had been applied with a shovel. She took absolutely no interest in James, instead her full attention was fixed on the man who sat opposite – an Italian opera singer called Eduardo Ponzi who was returning from a South American tour.

James had seen several posters around the ship announcing that the maestro would be performing a concert the following night – 'A performance of well-loved arias and popular Italian songs'.

'There is a small band on the *Colombie*,' Ponzi explained. 'They are not the finest musicians in the world, but I don't think that anyone will be paying them much attention. I could sing accompanied by barnyard animals and it would still be the finest concert you had ever heard!'

The Brazilian lady laughed too loudly and Ponzi acknowledged it with theatrical grace.

'It is marvellous that you will be honouring us with your singing, maestro,' she said.

'I sing for the love of it, *signora*. To me a day without song is like a day without food or drink . . . or love.'

Dumas leant over and whispered in James's ear.

'In truth he sings for free passage across the Atlantic.'

James stifled a laugh as the Brazilian woman gushed on.

'I just adore the Italian songs – they are so romantic. Do you know my favourite? "Funiculì, Funiculà."'

'Ah. But that is my favourite too, *signora*, I will dedicate it tomorrow night to you alone.' So saying Ponzi gave a brief and startlingly loud burst of the chorus.

'Ah,' said the Brazilian lady. 'Immediately I am in Italy, surrounded by beauty. I picture two young people walking hand in hand. I do not understand the words but the meaning is clear. It is a song about love.'

'Actually, *signora*,' said Ponzi, 'it is a song about a funicular railway.'

'No!'

'Yes! It was written to commemorate the opening of the first funicular railway on Mount Vesuvius.'

'Oh, I wish you hadn't told me that.'

This time James didn't hide his laughter, and soon everyone around him was joining in. Even the Brazilian woman.

As they were eating their dessert, a cream trifle stuffed with fruit and sherry, Signor Ponzi asked if anyone was interested in a game of bridge and Charmian's ears pricked up.

'James and I love to play,' she said. 'I think there is no better way to round off a meal than with a few rubbers of bridge.'

'Excellent,' said the maestro. 'I have only recently learned to play, but there is much sitting around on a musical tour and I am afraid that I have become rather an addict.'

'Do you have a partner?' Charmian asked.

'A French man I met on board,' said Ponzi. 'Emil Lefebvre.'

After dinner they retired to the lounge and were joined by Lefebvre. James studied him with interest. He had a waxed moustache and was elegantly dressed in what would be considered in England rather too flashy a manner. He wore a striped suit with matching tie and had a peach-coloured silk handkerchief sprouting from his top pocket like an exotic flower. A permanent half smile played on his lips and his liquid brown eyes sparkled as they greedily took everything in, missing nothing.

He made a great show of being gallant towards Charmian, kissing her hand and complimenting her on her dress. He suggested they make the game more interesting by swapping partners so that he could play with Charmian, but she insisted that she stay with James.

'It is only that my Italian friend might be the greatest singer in the world, by his reckoning at least,' said Emil, 'but he is far from being the greatest card player in the world. Forgive me, maestro, if I speak too plainly, but I think you will agree.'

JAMES LOVED THE GAME . . .

'I play for fun,' said Ponzi.

'Don't we all?' said Emil, 'but it is also pleasant to win now and again. By partnering the lovely Madame Bond I was merely trying to increase my chances.'

Emil leered at Charmian and all but winked. 'I sense, *madame*, that you are a tiger when it comes to the cards.'

'I don't know about that,' said Charmian coolly. 'But I *do* enjoy playing.'

James smiled. The Frenchman had been right. Charmian's looks disguised the fact that she was a tiger in so many ways, not just at cards. And she had a strong competitive streak. When it came to bridge she was utterly ruthless.

James loved the game, which his aunt had taught him. At its heart it was very simple, based on whist, in which the highest card played in the lead suit won the trick, with trump cards beating everything – but what made the game fascinating and complex was the bidding. At the start of each hand the players calculated how many tricks they thought they could win, and bid against each other to choose trumps. The team that bet they would win the most number of tricks won the bid. They then, of course, had to actually take those tricks to win the round. Bidding was an art and James felt that it would take a lifetime to master, for not only were you trying to calculate your own chances of winning, you had to also calculate what cards your partner might be holding, as well as the strength of the opposing team's hands. You relied heavily on how your partner played, and, as Charmian was very fond of telling him, many marriages had been destroyed over the bridge table.

The first couple of rounds went smoothly. Nobody was taking any risks as they tested the other players, and, as the cards snapped down on to the table, the four of them chatted amicably.

Emil told them that he was the manager of a French gymnastics team that was travelling back from a tournament in Venezuela. James had seen the men about the ship. Fifteen or so burly brutes who competed boisterously in all the games on deck and drank noisily in the bars at night.

Ponzi told a few humorous anecdotes from his life on the stage and played with enthusiasm and good spirit, but his bidding was all over the place. Charmian's experience made up for James's relative inexperience and Emil would have played better if he hadn't become gradually more and more annoyed and frustrated by the opera singer's mistakes. Gradually the banter died away and a tense atmosphere settled over the table.

Emil smoked powerful Turkish cigarettes continuously and ordered brandy after brandy from the steward. Slowly a poisonous mist seemed to form around him. It was obvious that Charmian and James were going to win and Emil's twinkly Gallic charm was replaced by a brooding surliness. A series of sharp remarks aimed at the maestro eventually turned into full-blown jibes.

'You idiot! What are you doing? How can you be so stupid? Only an imbecile would bid six no trumps with a hand like that!'

For his part the Italian kept his good nature and merely laughed and shrugged off Emil's insults.

At one point Emil grew so incensed it looked like he was going to physically assault his partner.

'Calm down, my friend!' Ponzi exclaimed, shaking his head with amusement. 'It is only a game of cards. You remind me of that other Frenchman they are holding below. The butcher Caiboche. I fear for my life!'

'What do you know of Caiboche?' said Emil. 'He is a soldier, you are a singer. You are from different worlds.'

'Please,' said Charmian, and she gave a theatrical shudder. 'I don't like to be reminded that we are sharing this ship with that monster. The captain was telling me at dinner that many of the passengers are complaining, and who can blame them? They ask him why Caiboche couldn't be kept out of the way in the hold, or somewhere. But the gendarmes apparently insisted on having proper quarters. Quite frankly, I don't think it would make the blindest bit of difference *where* he was on the ship, he could be down in the bilge water slopping about with the rats, for all I care – he would still be an evil presence.'

'I am interested that you use the word "*evil*", *madame*,' said Emil.

'And why not?'

'Caiboche is merely a soldier; would you call all solders evil?'

'I would not. And this man Caiboche was more than just a soldier.'

'The French government trained him to be a killer of men. In a war a man may kill thousands of enemy soldiers and be called a hero.'

'I don't approve of war either, to tell you the truth, Monsieur Lefebvre. But if Caiboche was at war in Algeria it was a war entirely of his own making.'

'So he killed some Algerians . . . are we to shed tears over a few filthy Arabs?'

James saw Charmian bristle.

'I would prefer you not to talk about the Arabs in that manner,' she said.

'I apologize if I have offended you,' said Emil. 'But I have travelled in North Africa and I can assure you the Arab is not to be trusted.'

'I have travelled in North Africa as well,' said Charmian. 'And I made an effort to get to know the people there. They are some of the most charming, civilized and honourable people I know.'

'Maybe I have just met the wrong sort of Arab,' Emil muttered.

'No matter what one thinks of the Algerians,' said Charmian, 'it would not excuse Caiboche his butchery.'

Emil shrugged. 'There are many in France who look up to him still. Who would not see him in chains and punished. There are many to whom he is still a hero. He has a great deal of respect among the French.'

'And I am sure that there are many Frenchmen who would see him hanged,' said Charmian.

Emil looked at Charmian through a veil of smoke.

'That is no way for a soldier to die.'

'It's a clean and a quick death at least,' said Charmian. 'Better that than dysentery, or having your guts torn out by a grenade.'

'No. I do not agree. A soldier should die in battle.'

'What do you suggest, then, *monsieur*?' said Charmian. 'That we stand Caiboche on a battlefield and send in the full force of the French army to cut him down?'

'I do not suggest anything,' said Emil. 'It is not up to me, *madame*.'

'Indeed. It is for the French courts to decide what becomes of the wretch.'

The game was nearly over and they were all waiting for Ponzi to play a card. The poor man had been deliberating endlessly, plucking at first one card and then another, to the annoyance of his partner.

James sat back in his chair and looked around the room. There were windows at the front and back. Those at the front looked into the ship's interior where there was an open concourse. Those at the rear looked out on to a smoking deck where a few hardy souls were wrapped in overcoats puffing away at cigars. As they were right at the stern of the ship there was nothing past the smoking deck but sea and sky and the faint trace of the ship's wash unspooling into the darkness behind them. The lounge itself was as lavishly decorated as the rest of the *Colombie* with painted wooden panels on the walls lit by pink glass wall lights. The panels showed classical scenes, with girls, nymphs and goddesses draped in flimsy silks that did nothing to hide their shape.

James looked at the faces of the girls, wondering what had become of the models they were based on. He then found himself staring at one that looked very familiar – was it possible he knew the model? It was a moment before he realized that it was a trick of the light. He was not looking at a painting but at a real living, breathing girl, and it was another moment before he realized that he did indeed know the person who the face belonged to. She was a year older, and had grown up since he had last seen her, but it was unmistakably someone from his past.

He shifted his position for a better look. The girl was talking to an older man as the two of them played cards together.

She had long blonde hair tied back with a silver clasp. James had only ever seen her before in riding clothes, but tonight she was wearing a smart dress that matched her eyes, which were the most vivid emerald green.

Wilder Lawless.

He had met her in Scotland last Easter when he had been visiting his dying uncle. She lived for horses and had rescued James from a crazy American arms manufacturer who had been intent on killing him.

What was she doing on board and why hadn't he seen her before now? He ached for the game to be finished so that he could go over and talk to her, but the last hand still had to be played out.

The rest of the game was an agony. Ponzi seemed to be playing slower and slower, and now he was beginning to annoy James as well as Emil.

At last the ordeal was over. Emil ground out his cigarette and thanked them gracelessly before launching into a drunken tirade against the hapless Italian.

James made his excuses and hurried over to Wilder's table, calling out her name.

Wilder looked up with a bland expression on her face that turned into a look of surprise, and then her face flushed scarlet and exploded into a brilliant smile. She jumped up and hugged him.

'James!'

'What on earth are you doing here?' they both said together.

'I've been in Mexico with my aunt,' said James. 'How about you?'

'I'm working with my father now,' she explained and nodded towards the man she had been playing cards with. It turned out that Robert Lawless had a new job, transporting horses across the Atlantic from South America.

'Up until now I've spent the whole voyage down in the hold with six Argentinian ponies,' Wilder told him. 'Settling them down. I've been doing shifts with Dad. When I've not been there I've been eating and sleeping in my cabin. I hate to see them so distressed, but I've learned how to make them feel comfortable enough and not afraid. Oh, James, what a lovely surprise it is to see you!'

Mr Lawless saw that they wanted to catch up with each other's news so after some small talk he left them to it and turned in for the night.

James and Wilder sat there for the next two hours chatting away. James was amazed at how much older and more mature Wilder seemed. She was becoming a young woman. He supposed he must have grown up too.

'The last time we met I seem to remember your way of making friends was to wrestle me to the ground,' she said and now it was James's turn to blush.

'Oh, don't remind of me of that,' said James. 'You never did like being thought of as a mere girl.'

'No. And that hasn't changed.'

'And you obviously still love horses. Do you still have Martini? Where is he?'

'Back in England,' said Wilder. 'We live on a farm in Devon now. It's not as wet as Scotland and there aren't any midges, but I still miss the old country. And I *really* miss Martini when I'm away, which is a lot.' Wilder paused as a thought came to her and her face lit up. 'Would you like to meet the horses?'

James had no real desire to meet a horse, South American or otherwise, but he didn't want to offend Wilder, and besides it would be a chance to have a look round a different part of the ship.

'I'd love to,' he said.

'Tomorrow, then. We'll go down after dinner before the concert begins. I suppose you're going to the concert?'

'I suppose I shall have to,' said James. 'I've just spent the last hour playing cards with the great maestro himself. But what are you up to tomorrow during the day? Are you busy with the horses all the time?'

'No, they're settled in now. Dad will check on them in the morning.'

'Then we can have the whole day together?' said James.

Wilder looked at him and smiled.

'That would be lovely,' she said.

James smiled back. Things were looking up. The rest of the voyage was going to be a lot more fun than he had expected.

The next day started sunny and warm, but as the *Colombie* steamed on ever northwards the sky clouded, the sea turned grey and a light drizzle sprang up, turning the decks wet and slippery. It was almost as if at this halfway point some over-officious rain god had decided that now was the time for some British weather. Being with Wilder helped remind James that not everything about his home country was dull and cold, though. Her smile could make the darkest of days bright.

The two of them were inseparable. They talked and talked. If anyone had asked James later what they had talked about, however, he wouldn't have been able to say. As they chatted they walked around the deck, joined in some outdoor games, ate lunch, stood at the rail watching the foam and the spray as the ship cut through the waves, played cards in the salon, or simply sat in deck chairs in the rain, laughing at how wet they were getting.

In the afternoon they met the first officer, Dumas, who showed them around the bridge. Then they ate dinner together and, finally, it was time to go down into the hold and visit the horses.

They descended from the lavishly decorated upper decks, with their patterned carpets and flocked wallpaper hung with paintings of seascapes, past the first-class cabins, then the second-class, right to the lowest level. There were no decorations down here. The passageways were narrow, with paint flaking off the ironwork. Wilder knew exactly where she was going and confidently led James through the rabbit warren of corridors as if she had done it a thousand times before. They came eventually to a metal door set into the wall on their right and Wilder knocked. Presently the door was opened by a fat red-faced man whose white moustache matched his white French Line uniform. He had a bored, sleepy look about him, accentuated by two droopy eyes and a great hanging bulb of a nose. He gave a sort of welcoming shrug to Wilder and she asked him in fluent French if he would let her into the hold. He nodded and ducked back into his office before returning a moment later with a clipboard and a large set of keys. He slowly and lugubriously got Wilder and James to sign their names before dropping the clipboard on a shelf just inside his door. He put on a saggy well-worn cap and shuffled along the passageway through a bulkhead and up to a much larger door. He spun the locking handle and pushed the door open, all with slow careful movements. He then sighed and stood aside to let the two of them go through before closing the door behind them.

'Louis is used to me now,' Wilder explained. 'The first few times I had to show him all sorts of official letters and forms and permissions. He doesn't bother with all that any more, thank goodness. It used to take an age.'

They were on the floor of the hold, threading their way between the cargo that was stored here. On all sides were trunks, crates and packing cases. This was a passenger vessel rather than a freight ship but it still carried a large amount of goods. As well as luggage and belongings being shipped back by passengers there was commercial freight.

Before he saw the horses James heard a grunt and a whinny. They had evidently smelt Wilder.

'The poor devils,' she said. 'They hate it down here. I keep trying to tell them it's only for a few days, but they're South American horses – they don't speak English.'

James knew that Wilder was joking, but he still felt uncomfortable when people treated animals as if they were humans, with the same thoughts and emotions.

The six horses were standing in small stalls along the rear of the hold. Their great long heads looked out over the gates with sad expressions, though one tossed its mane and snorted as Wilder approached him and stroked his nose.

'He's a criollo,' Wilder explained. 'A South American breed, descended from horses brought over by the conquistadors. They're clever animals. Very reliable. Very strong. These lads are going to Spain. A nobleman near Cadiz wants to try breeding with them. Aren't they beautiful?'

James looked at them. He had never really trusted horses. They all looked slightly mad to him. He thought it best not to say anything to Wilder, though, knowing how much she loved the animals.

'They're certainly handsome,' he said.

'It's all right. I've always known you're not a horse person,' said Wilder. 'Despite the fact that Martini saved your life that time.'

'In fairness, Wilder,' said James. 'It was you that saved my life. You may have been riding Martini at the time, but left to his own devices I don't think he would have come to my rescue.'

'When a good horseman is mounted, James, then horse and rider are one.'

'A little like a good driver at the wheel of a car,' said James. 'Give me a car any day. I never did see eye to eye with horses.'

'It's nothing like being behind the wheel of a dirty smelly old car, James.'

'We shall have to agree to differ.'

As they talked Wilder busied herself with the horses – checking their feed, changing their straw, looking over their big powerful bodies for any signs of distress. The horses could move around a little in their stalls and she had to be sure that none of them had hurt themselves. She refilled their water and combed through the tangled mane of one of them, a chestnut stallion with a white flash on its chest.

James helped as best he could, but kept a wary distance from the animals. In his experience they could kick out without warning, and their big teeth looked like they could take a sizeable chunk out of you.

It was while they were working away and chatting that James became aware of footsteps and voices. The two of them were in one of the stalls spreading clean straw and James instinctively fell silent. He looked along the length of the hold and caught sight of Emil Lefebvre with two other men.

James raised a hand to Wilder. Something about Emil's furtive manner had alerted him. There would no doubt be a perfectly innocent explanation for him being down here, but James didn't trust the smooth French man.

'What's the matter?' Wilder whispered.

'Probably nothing,' said James. 'But let's just keep quiet and see what they're up to.'

The two men with Emil could not have been more different from each other. One was a lot younger, somewhere in his early twenties. He was short and stocky and walked on the balls of his feet in a sort of cartoon bounce. His long arms hung motionless at his sides and he was carrying two sturdy canvas holdalls. The other man was older and taller, with long silver-grey hair pushed back from a balding head. He had very prominent features – a fat nose, a jutting chin, a heavy brow and large ears. From his thick drooping lower lip hung a cigarette. His dark-tanned skin was rough and pockmarked.

As they came nearer James heard them talking in French.

'How will we find them among all this junk?' said the stocky one.

'They are well marked,' said Emil. 'And stamped fragile. So there should be nothing stacked on top of them. Ah, *voilà*! What did I tell you? You should trust me, Maury.'

The stocky young man, Maury, shrugged and nodded. 'I *do* trust you, Emil,' he said, and the three of them walked over to where two matching crates were sitting on top of some packing cases, secured in place with a large cargo net.

'Help me with this, Argente,' said Maury, unfastening the guy ropes from the net, which was attached to rings in the floor. The silver-haired man, Argente, gave him a hand, his cigarette still dangling from his lip. They soon had the net off and Maury jumped up on to the packing cases.

'Pass me the magic key,' he said to Argente and the silver-haired man opened one of the canvas bags. He fished out a crowbar and handed it up to Maury. There was the screech of nails being pulled from wood as Maury eased the lid off a crate.

'Poof!' He grimaced and flapped his hand in front of his face. Evidently something in the case smelt bad. Then Maury smiled.

'Ah,' he said. 'A pretty sight. Sleeping like babies.'

Argente, meanwhile, had climbed up, taken the crowbar and opened the second, much smaller, crate. He nodded and pushed a hand through his hair.

'*Bien*.' He jumped down and Maury followed.

'We will carry everything up to the cabin now,' said Emil. 'The concert will be starting in twenty minutes. The *Perceval* will be alongside at half past ten. So we have nearly two hours. I think this will be enough. *Maintenant, vite.*'

Maury and Argente climbed back up with the holdalls and began loading them with items from the first crate.

The holdalls were soon full and James watched as the two men handed them carefully down to Emil. They looked heavy.

'We will have to make two journeys,' said Emil. 'Argente, you come with me. Maury, you stay behind and watch the stuff.'

'OK, boss,' said Maury and he sat down on a packing case and lit a cigarette, the crowbar at his side.

Wilder and James were still crouching behind the stall door, peering out through a narrow gap. Wilder looked at James and they moved back into the rear of the stall behind the horse, where it was darker.

'I think we've seen something we shouldn't have,' Wilder whispered.

'It could be nothing,' said James.

'What were they unpacking?'

'I'm not sure. I couldn't see. Let's just stay quiet and hidden, and when they've all gone we'll say something to one of the ship's officers.'

'Or to Louis,' Wilder murmured. 'He must have let them in.'

'Maybe,' said James, but before they could say anything more they heard voices again and James shifted back to the door to take a look.

It was Louis. He had come into the hold and was gesticulating angrily at Maury, who was acting very nonchalant.

'You should not be in here!' Louis was shouting. 'And smoking a cigarette! Are you crazy? You will set fire to the whole ship.'

Maury muttered something and crushed his cigarette out with the heel of his boot.

Now Louis was looking at the opened crates.

'Have you opened these?'

'They are our crates,' said Maury. 'We needed to check something.'

'You are not allowed in here during the voyage and you are not allowed to open any cargo between customs. This is not acceptable. I will need to inform the captain.'

'I was not to know,' said Maury, and he smiled at Louis. 'Come now, I didn't mean any harm. You don't need to say anything. I will put everything back how it was and nobody will ever know. And how about I give you a little something for your trouble?'

Maury moved his hand inside his jacket as if to take his wallet out. Louis made a dismissive noise and shook his head.

'How did you get in here?' he asked.

'The door was open,' said Maury. 'We were going to ask permission but when we saw that it was unlocked we just came through. We thought it was no big deal.'

'Crazy,' Louis mumbled, then nodded towards the crates. 'What is in there, anyway?'

'Sports equipment, for the team, that is all.'

Louis sighed. 'I will need to take a look.'

'Be my guest.'

Maury got to his feet and helped Louis up on to the packing case. As Louis leant over to inspect the contents, however, Maury snatched up the crowbar and swung it at the back of his head, knocking him off the case and on to the floor.

Louis landed heavily and gave a horrible groan of pain. He clutched his head in his hands, blood pouring between his fingers.

'*Fou*,' said Maury and he hopped down. He stood over Louis and raised the crowbar to strike again.

James couldn't watch it happen. Louis was already badly injured. Another blow from the iron bar would be fatal. James was out of the stall and moving swift and silent across the hold as soon as Maury's back was turned. As the Frenchman lifted the bar, the vicious curved end dropping back over his shoulder, James grabbed it and wrenched it free.

MAURY SNATCHED UP THE CROWBAR AND SWUNG IT
AT THE BACK OF HIS HEAD . . .

Maury gave a colourful Gallic curse and spun on his heel. He looked amazed to see a boy standing there wielding his crowbar, and he looked even more amazed when James deftly flipped the tool and neatly caught it the other way round, ready for action.

Maury's response was to reach inside his jacket, as he had done before. Instead of bringing out a wallet, however, he brought out a slim fisherman's knife used for gutting fish – just as useful for gutting a human being. He tossed it mockingly from hand to hand like a juggler.

'I don't know who you are,' he said, 'or what you think you are doing, but you have five seconds to put down that *pied-de-biche* before I gut you like a mackerel.'

'The name's Bond, James Bond. And you've got four seconds to put down that knife before I break your hand.'

Maury snorted and gave James a withering look.

'Well, come on, then,' said James. 'Do you want to start counting, or shall I?'

Maury frowned, trying to get the measure of this boy. Then he lunged at James without warning. Stabbing the knife forward.

James was ready for him; he stepped to the side and swung the crowbar. It hit Maury in the wrist, who yelped and dropped the knife. James moved in quickly, dropped the bar, took hold of Maury in a judo hold and before the startled young man knew what was happening James had turned him and dropped him on to his back, knocking the fight out of him.

Maury lay there for a moment, stunned, but he quickly pulled himself together and he was just reaching out for his knife when Wilder dropped the cargo net over him.

'Good thinking,' said James.

'For a girl,' said Wilder.

'You said it, not me,' said James, and, while Maury was still confused by this sudden turn of events, they rolled him up in the net and tied the guy ropes round him so that he couldn't move.

He wriggled and swore and shouted, but he was going nowhere.

James picked up the fallen knife and slipped it into the back of his belt. Wilder went to Louis. He was lying on his side, holding his head. He was very weak and had a dazed, distant look about him, but he was still conscious and the flow of blood had stemmed to a dribble.

'There's a first-aid box on the wall,' said Wilder, pointing, and James hurried over to it. 'And bring some water.'

In a couple of minutes they had roughly bandaged Louis's head and laid him comfortably out of the way on some straw. James tried not to rush it, but he was all too aware that Emil and Argente might return at any minute.

'We need to see what's in those crates,' he said, and they clambered up on to the packing cases.

The smaller crate was full of boxes of bullets and coiled ammunition belts packed in straw.

James whistled. 'Well, they're obviously not a gymnastics team,' he said. 'Unless the sport's changed somewhat since I've been away. Looks like they're planning to start a war.'

'I suppose the other crate's full of guns,' said Wilder.

'One way to find out.'

The men had emptied most of the contents of the first crate they'd opened, but there were still two broken-down rifles lying on a bed of straw. There was something underneath them, and the smell was awful. It stuck in James's throat.

'Do you suppose they hid the guns among some meat or something?' said Wilder, covering her nose and mouth.

'You might not want to look,' said James.

'Oh, don't start with all that again,' said Wilder. 'The poor wee lassie can't mess about with man's things.'

'Have it your own way,' said James and he reached into the crate. He lifted out the rifles and pulled the straw to one side.

Wilder gasped, clamped her hand tight over her face and swayed on her feet. James swallowed hard. He felt bile rise in his throat and a chill grip his insides.

There was a man's dead body lying there. His face was bloated and purple. The swollen tongue protruding from his mouth. He was wearing some kind of officer's uniform. Something naval, perhaps, though James didn't recognize it. He had been tied up and his throat had been slit. James reckoned he knew whose knife had been used.

'Poor devil,' said James. 'I wonder who he is.'

'I'm not staying to find out,' said Wilder. 'We have to get out of here before they come back.'

James knocked his fist against his forehead, trying to think.

'We've got to stop them before they kill anyone else,' he said.

'What? You and me?' said Wilder. 'Are you out of your mind? What can we do?'

'We have to do something. Once they're armed they're going to be very dangerous.'

'They already *are* armed,' said Wilder. 'They took two full bags of guns with them.'

'Yes,' said James, jumping down and running over to the stalls, 'but they didn't take anything from the other crate.'

'What are you suggesting?'

'If we take the bullets their guns will be useless,' said James, hurrying back with a sack he'd spotted earlier.

'But, James —'

'Shut up and help me load them into this.'

They quickly lifted out the ammunition and packed it into the sack, working in silence, listening for any sound of the returning Frenchmen.

'What will we do with it all?' asked Wilder as she crammed the last box of bullets in.

'We'll hide it somewhere.'

'Where?'

'I don't know . . . somewhere. That's enough questions. We need to hurry.'

Fear was making James short-tempered and rude, but he'd worry about apologizing to Wilder later.

If there was a later . . .

He hefted the sack on to his shoulder. It weighed a ton and the sharp wooden boxes dug into his back. Just in case, he told Wilder to bring the crowbar.

They cautiously moved towards the exit, ready to hide if they heard anything. Halfway there James had to stop and put the sack down for a moment.

'Let me help you with that,' said Wilder. James was about to say something to put her off but immediately thought better of it.

'Thanks,' he said and they carried it between them. It was still heavy going and before they could get safely out they heard approaching footsteps. James dragged Wilder and the sack behind a tower of steamer trunks and they stood there, still as corpses, hardly daring to breathe as Emil and Argente hurried past, trailing tobacco smoke.

Once they were sure it was safe James and Wilder emerged from their hiding place and shuffled as quickly as they could to the exit. Soon they heard shouting from over by the stalls and they broke into a clumsy, staggering run, at any moment expecting to hear someone coming after them.

They got out and James slammed the door shut. He spun the wheel that kept it closed and jammed the crowbar into it.

'That might slow them down for a few minutes,' said James, 'but we need to keep moving.'

They clattered along the passageway, panting and gasping with the effort, and looked into Louis's little office. Empty.

'We don't have a lot of time,' said James. 'We need to get help.'

'Aye.'

They climbed up through the ship's interior towards the top deck, hoping to stumble across someone. But the *Colombie* seemed deserted.

'Everyone must be at the concert,' said James, gasping with the effort of dragging the heavy sack. 'Or sheltering from the rain.'

'What will we do?' asked Wilder.

'I'll hide this lot somewhere; you look for a member of the crew,' said James. 'Head for the bridge if you can't find an officer on duty. Tell them what's happened. And tell them to be careful. God knows what Emil and his cronies are up to, but if we act quickly they're not going to get very far.'

'Can you manage with that heavy bag, James?'

'I'll have to.'

They had reached the top deck and emerged, panting, into the rain-sodden air. James hefted the sack on to his shoulder and tried not to wince at the weight of it. He gave Wilder a reassuring smile and they split up. James marched stiff-legged towards the stern, trying not to slip over. Wilder dashed off in the opposite direction.

It was dark and there was nobody else on deck. The thin strains of distant music rose from below. The concert had started. Everyone apart from the crew would be watching.

James had no clear plan of where he was going to hide the ammunition. There were a thousand and one places on board. But he had to choose somewhere nobody would think of, and he had to choose fast. There were at least fifteen men in Emil's phoney 'gymnastics' team. They might already be searching the ship.

As James plodded along, sagging under the weight of the sack, he looked everywhere for a suitable spot – behind the lifeboats, in the ventilator cowlings, under benches – and then it struck him.

What an idiot he was!

He had the best hiding place in the world. Somewhere things once hidden could never be found again.

Summoning his last few ounces of strength he hauled the sack over to the railing and somehow managed to hoist it up so that it rested on the top. He took a deep breath and shoved it off. It kept pace with the ship as it dropped down the side, then it hit the black water of the Atlantic with an inaudible splash and disappeared.

James rested a while at the railing, enjoying a brief moment of calm and peace. Standing here, looking at the great rolling mass of the ocean, the events of the last half an hour seemed unreal. As long as he had been busy he hadn't realized how frightened he was. How close to death he must have been. Now the fear and the tension came flooding in on him and he felt a second's dizziness. He needed to rest for a minute and get his nerve back, and then he would go and find Wilder. After all, Maury would have told Emil and Argente what had happened. He would have given them a description of his attackers. It was only a matter of time before they got out of the hold.

Come on, James. You can't hang around here like a shop dummy. The danger's not over yet.

He turned and headed back in the direction that Wilder had gone in. He pushed all thoughts of the men and what they might be up to into the back of his mind to let his subconscious mull it over. He switched off the thinking part of his brain and relied on instinct.

As he ran down the promenade deck he almost collided with an crew member coming out of a door. It was Dumas, the first officer. He looked flustered.

'Ah, James,' he said in his heavily accented English. 'Thank God I found you. I was searching everywhere. Follow me.'

Dumas ducked back inside.

'Where are we going?'

'I found the girl, Miss Lawless. At first I didn't know what she was babbling about.'

'But you believe her?'

'But of course. Why would someone make up a story like that? I have sent someone to inform the captain, who is at the concert. For now you must come with me. We must put you safely out of the way.'

'And Wilder?'

'Do not worry, *mon brave*, I am taking you to her. We must hurry, though. And watch out for any danger!'

Dumas checked to see that there was no one about before rattling down an iron stairway. At the bottom he turned towards the rear of the ship and led James along a corridor to the open concourse outside the lounge.

Dumas went over to the lounge door and knocked twice. James noticed that the curtains in all the windows were drawn.

'You will be safe in here,' said Dumas, and once again he looked both ways before unlocking the door with his pass key.

He stood aside to let James enter.

'After you,' he said and smiled at James, his teeth showing white against the blue-grey of his jaw.

James stepped inside and for a moment could make no sense of the scene that awaited him. Then a shove from behind sent him sprawling fully into the lounge where he steadied himself against a chair. He looked back. Dumas was coming in, it must have been him who had pushed James.

James felt a horrible deflation.

Emil was sitting at a table. Argente was standing by a leather settee where Wilder was slumped, looking utterly dejected. Maury was sitting next to her, one bandaged hand draped over her shoulders. Three of the 'gymnastics team' stood by the doors to the smoking deck at the rear.

'It was not difficult,' said Dumas in French, locking the door. 'He was up on deck.'

'And the bullets?'

'I don't know. He did not have them with him. I thought it was best to get him out of the way before I asked.'

Emil sighed and stroked some fluff off his jacket. 'I don't know what you were thinking of, James,' he said, switching to English. 'Acting the hero. Did you think this was just a game? As harmless as a rubber of bridge?'

James sat down in the chair so that they wouldn't see his legs trembling.

'No,' he said. 'I knew it wasn't a game. Certainly not with the sort of toys you have.' He glanced over at Emil's table where there were fifteen or so guns laid out in neat rows. Rifles, pistols, even a couple of sub-machine guns.

'They are not toys,' said Emil.

'They might as well be without any bullets,' said James.

At that Emil got up, calmly walked across the carpet and slapped James hard in the face.

James was so full of adrenalin and excitement he hardly felt it. But Wilder gasped.

'Where are the bullets?' Emil asked, taking his handkerchief from his pocket and wiping his lips.

'I've hidden them,' said James. 'Somewhere you will never find them.'

'You didn't have long. We know where you were. We will find them eventually.'

'In time?' said James.

'There is no hurry.'

'Isn't there? I thought you had to get this over with before the concert finishes.'

'Why don't you just tell us where the bullets are now and you can live a long and happy life,' said Emil wearily. 'If you do not tell us then I am afraid your life will be short and miserable.'

'Short and miserable it is, then,' said James. 'But I'm not going to tell you and time is running out. You have until half past ten. Then your getaway boat arrives.'

'It will not take me long to force the information out of you. Everyone has a weak spot.'

'Really? How can you be so sure of that?'

'Because you are just a boy, and I know how to hurt you in a thousand ways.'

'Go on, then,' said James, sounding braver than he felt.

Once again Emil slapped him. Harder this time. Hard enough to knock James out of his chair. His head was stinging, his mouth bleeding, and he spat blood on to the carpet.

'I'm not going to tell you anything,' he said.

'What about the girl, then?' Emil walked over to the sofa.

'She doesn't know anything,' said James. 'I didn't tell her where I was going to hide the ammunition. Leave her alone.'

'Ah, we have found your weak spot,' said Emil. 'That did not take long, did it?'

Emil laughed and James felt a hot flush of helpless anger burn across his cheeks.

'We don't have to hurt you, after all,' said Emil, taking off his jacket and rolling up his shirtsleeves. The other men were laughing too now.

'I wonder how long can you sit there and watch while we have our fun with her,' said Emil, lifting Wilder's chin with his hand.

'Perhaps we could start by cutting her pretty face. And then . . .'

'All right,' said James. 'I'll talk.'

'Don't tell them anything!' Wilder shouted.

'It's no use,' said James. 'I'm not going to see you hurt.'

He looked at Emil.

'If you promise not to harm her in any way I'll take you to where the bullets are.'

'James, no . . .'

'We did our best, Wilder,' said James, 'but in the end this is nothing to do with us.'

'Your best was not good enough, was it?' said Emil. 'After all, you are only children.'

'We don't have time for talk,' said Dumas, checking his watch. 'Get the bullets now. We must arm the men.'

Emil glanced at his own watch.

'*Oui*. I will go with him to make sure there are no mistakes this time.' He shot an accusing look at Maury on the sofa, put his jacket back on and nodded at James.

'Get moving, boy.'

'Just remember that your girlfriend is waiting for you back there,' said Emil as James led him up on to the promenade deck.

'I won't forget,' said James.

'Her mistake was to go straight to Dumas,' said Emil. 'He was keeping watch for us on deck. He is not the only crew member on board who is loyal to our cause.'

'Your cause?'

'*Bien sûr.*'

'Let me take a guess,' said James. 'You're hoping to free General Caiboche and get him away to safety on another ship – the *Perceval.*'

'Do you expect me to pat you on the head and call you a clever boy, James?'

'Not really, no. I expect you to give me a long boring speech about how great Caiboche is and how feeble I am.'

'No speeches,' said Emil. 'We are all soldiers. We prefer to act rather than to talk.'

'I thought even soldiers knew the difference between civilians and other soldiers. Or do you not care who you kill?'

'The only matter of any importance is that we free Caiboche.'

'And if a few passengers get in the way and end up floating face down in the Atlantic? What does that matter to the butcher of Aziz?'

'If we can avoid violence we will,' said Emil. 'There is no point in wasting bullets. We will simply smash the ship's radio and do enough damage to stop her engines for a few hours. The *Perceval* is fast. We will be well away from here before anyone else has any idea what has happened.'

'Is Caiboche really worth all this trouble?'

'He is a great man,' said Emil. 'A great *général*. His day has not yet come, but he will be a new Napoleon.'

'It might be well to remember,' said James, 'that the British beat Napoleon and he died in exile, a British prisoner.'

Emil cuffed James round the back of the head.

'Enough,' he said. 'Where is the ammunition?'

They had been walking along the rain-slick deck, and James's mind had been working away at his problem. And it was still a very big problem. By bringing Emil up here had he done nothing more than buy himself a few minutes?

No. He had reduced the odds. In the lounge it had been seven against one – two if you counted Wilder, although at the moment she was more of a hindrance than a help.

Out here on deck it was one against one. Admittedly it was one man – a trained soldier – against a boy, but James had been up against worst odds in his time and come out on top. Also there was the advantage that they were in the open now. In public. Emil would have to be very careful what he did in full view of other passengers.

Other passengers? That was a joke.

It was like a ghost ship, the *Marie Celeste*.

The distant sound of music coming from the dining room reminded James that most of the passengers were watching Signor Ponzi. Emil and his men had timed the rescue attempt carefully and the rain and chilly air were helping them still further by keeping any passengers who were not at the concert below decks.

The crew would still be on duty, of course. How many of them, though, were in on the rescue attempt? As Emil had told Charmian last night, there were many in France who supported Caiboche.

They arrived at the spot where James had thrown the sack overboard. He was tempted to tell Emil what he had done, just to see the look on his face, but knew that wouldn't achieve very much. He wondered if the plan he had formulated would achieve any more. It was all he had managed to come up with in the short time available, and, like all such plans, it was very risky.

Was Emil armed in some way? Out in in plain sight like this he could hardly wave a weapon around, but James remembered all too well how Maury had been carrying a concealed knife. Emil would surely have one too.

If so, how long would it take him to get it out and use it?

Not long at all.

James told himself that these men had to be scared, despite their show of bravado. He had upset their careful plans. Without any bullets their guns were useless and their attack on the armed gendarmes would fail. It was nearly ten o'clock already. They had a strict timetable and would be getting very panicky.

James was in charge. He held all the cards. He could control events.

And the men had made one very big mistake.

He took a deep breath and felt a calm settle over him. He would let things play out, as if he were watching a film. There was an old familiar fluttering in his guts.

It was the calm before violent action.

He was ready.

'There,' he said.

'What?'

'I hid the ammunition under there.' James was pointing towards a lifeboat. Underneath it was a pool of inky darkness.

Emil squatted down for a better look.

'I can't see anything.'

'I pushed it right to the back.'

The rain had picked up and was lashing the deck.

'You get it,' said Emil, viewing the damp and slippery boards with distaste.

'All right.'

'And hurry up. I am getting soaked.'

Don't want to get your precious suit dirty, do you? thought James.

'I will be watching you,' Emil snapped. 'So don't try and do anything stupid.'

I won't, thought James, dropping on to his hands and knees. *I'm going to try and do something clever.*

He peered under the lifeboat. It was filthy and stank of the sea. He lay on his belly and wriggled in just far enough so that he was partially hidden from Emil.

In their panic and haste the men hadn't bothered to search James. They wouldn't expect him to be carrying any weapons, after all. But he still had Maury's knife under his jacket, slotted into the belt at the back of his trousers. It was a miracle he hadn't injured himself when he had fallen from the chair in the lounge.

First he needed to distract Emil.

'Did you serve with Caiboche?' he asked. 'In Africa?'

'Of course. We all served under him in the Legion except Argente, who knew him from his days in Marseilles. Now hurry!'

While they were talking James had slipped a hand under his jacket and eased the knife out. Now he gripped it firmly. He had to shorten his odds still further, though. If Emil's hands were full he wouldn't be able to get any weapon of his own out in a hurry.

'It's too heavy,' said James, taking hold of a rope with his free hand and trying to sound as if he were struggling. 'Grab hold of my legs and give me a pull, can you?'

He heard Emil curse then felt the man's hands about his ankles.

'Pull!'

James took a deep breath and held on tight to the rope for a second or so.

Now for it.

He let go.

Emil pulled hard and James shot out from under the lifeboat. Emil staggered back, thrown off balance, and James twisted round so that he was facing the right way up.

He swung the knife in a short fierce arc, stabbing downwards.

There was a *thunk* as the thin, vicious blade sliced though Emil's shoe leather, on through the soft skin, between the long bones of his foot, and right through the sole into the wooden deck. Pinning the Frenchman in place like a butterfly in a display.

Emil howled and let go of James.

James rolled on to his feet, belted Emil hard in the stomach and ran for it.

It had all happened too fast for Emil, and the pain was so shocking that he didn't immediately react. By the time he thought of dragging the pistol from his jacket pocket, James had gone.

There was no going back now. James had to see this through. Wilder was in real danger. He needed to get help. He couldn't trust any of the crew, but he knew who he *could* trust. The French gendarmes who were guarding Caiboche.

They would know what to do. If they acted fast they could overwhelm the six men in the lounge and get Wilder out before she came to any harm.

He bolted along the deck and ducked into the first open door he came to. He knew his way around the ship very well now and in less than a minute he was running along the corridor where they were holding Caiboche.

There . . .

No. Maybe he was mistaken. There were always two men on guard outside. Had he come to the wrong level?

No. He was sure of it. He looked up and down. Suite 3. That was the number. He sighed in frustration and hammered on the door. If it were the wrong cabin he'd soon find out.

There was no reply from within. He hammered again, and then tried the handle. It was unlocked. He pushed the door. It wouldn't open fully. Something was blocking it on the other side. He thrust it hard until there was a wide enough gap for him to squeeze through, and then stepped inside. He was in a little hallway not much larger than a cubicle. The light was off and he could find no switch. The half open door was blocking most of the light from the corridor. He could see enough to tell, though, that what was blocking the door was a man's lifeless body, and the floor was sticky with his blood.

James took a deep breath and ventured further into the suite. The next room was a small sitting room. The gendarmes had been living in here and it was a mess. There were overflowing ashtrays, magazines and newspapers strewn everywhere, the remains of a meal on the low table.

And two more dead men, their bodies grotesquely broken and twisted.

James didn't look too closely. They had been butchered. There were scarlet splashes on the carpet and up the walls.

James swayed as a wave of dizziness washed over him. His blood felt cold and sluggish in his veins. His heart laboured to pump it round his body.

He went through to the next room.

The dining room.

Another dead body, slumped against one wall, a long smear of gore running down the wallpaper in a thick red stripe, as if someone had thrown a wet sponge against it.

And there, at the far end of a polished wooden table, wearing only a bloody vest, his white skin tufted with jet-black hair.

Caiboche.

He was a man of rectangles, there was nothing rounded about him. His head was a solid square brick sitting on a wide square neck. His hair had been cut with a flat top and shaved sides that accentuated the squareness. At first James thought he had no ears, but then he realized they were so small and flat as to be almost invisible from the front. His squashed nose was an oblong lump on the front of his pale, expressionless face. His mouth a square letterbox showing small even teeth. Square jaw. Square body. His hands, lying still in small puddles of blood, were square slabs with short blunt fingers.

He wasn't a large man, but he seemed to fill the room and suck

all the oxygen and light out of it, so that it felt darker and more cramped than it really was. There was an eerie stillness about him as he sat there, staring unblinking at James, his forearms resting on the tabletop. His stillness somehow made him appear more powerful than if he'd been pacing the room flexing his muscles. There was a sense of tremendous stored-up energy, ready to burst out, so that the air seemed to pulse around the man, charged by his latent power.

His voice, when it came, was strangely gentle and soft, high-pitched, almost feminine. It belonged to a different man. But it was nevertheless mesmerizing.

'Who are you?'

'A passenger.'

'Why have you come in here?'

'The door was open.'

'I was expecting someone else.'

'Did you kill all these men?'

'They bored me.'

'And all those people in Africa? Did they bore you, too?'

'You haven't answered my question, boy. Who are you?'

James didn't intend to answer him. He was planning his moment, and now he took it. He lunged for the door.

Caiboche came to life and moved so quickly and so suddenly that James was taken completely by surprise. One moment the general was sitting there still as a statue, the next he had sprung to his feet and somehow thrown the table to one side. James hadn't understood how immensely strong the man was. The table hit the wall and splintered, and Caiboche powered forward like a charging rhino.

James was just ahead of him, out of the door and running. But in his panic he chose the wrong way out of the sitting room and found himself in a bedroom. He didn't stop, but careered on and into the bathroom. Where he turned and locked the door.

Caiboche crashed into the door from the other side and it shuddered but didn't break. It was made of heavy mahogany. There was a second crash, then silence.

James pressed his back against the door in a feeble attempt to make it hold firm and waited for the next assault. This one would surely break the lock.

For a long while nothing happened. James found himself staring at the shower curtain, which was drawn across the bath. It didn't immediately register with him that this was odd.

And then he was sure he saw it twitch.

'Is there somebody there?' he whispered.

'*Oui.*'

A moment later a familiar face appeared round the end of the curtain. It was the young French adjutant, René Mathis, his face white with fear.

'René?' said James, keeping his voice as low as possible. 'Thank God you're all right. What are you doing in here?'

'I am hiding from that monster.'

'What happened?'

'For days he did not move. He sat there, staring at the clock. We got careless. Eventually we left him alone, for half a minute, no more, and somehow he slipped his chains. He was like a wild animal. In five minutes all the others were dead. In the confusion I managed to hide in here. I did not even dare to lock the door in case he heard me. Every moment I expected him to come and find me and . . . It was awful what he did to the others. He is not human.'

James swallowed hard. 'Do you have a weapon?' he said.

'I have my revolver,' said René. 'I had no chance to use it, though. You must think me an awful coward.'

'Not at all,' said James. 'Aren't I hiding in here with you myself?'

'But you are not a policeman.'

'Well there are several policemen out there,' said James quietly, 'and probably very brave ones, too, but they are also very dead policemen. You're more use alive, René. Maybe the two of us can overpower him.'

'*Non.* Our only hope is to shoot and shoot fast, and keep on shooting.'

'Do you feel up to trying?'

'Not really. But I think we have no choice.'

'You get your gun ready,' said James. 'I'll unlock the door. OK?'

'OK.'

'Be ready to fire as soon as I pull it open,' said James. 'He won't be expecting that.'

'You sound like you know a lot about his sort of thing.'

'I've had a little practice . . . Ready?'

Mathis nodded and James quietly slipped the lock.

Mathis knelt and aimed his pistol at the door, steadying his arm with his free hand. James could see the gun shaking in time with Mathis's racing pulse.

'Three . . . two . . . one . . .'

James pulled the door open in one clean, swift movement. He tensed himself for the shot.

None came.

'Well?'

'I cannot see him.'

James moved around behind the kneeling gendarme.

The bedroom looked empty.

'He could be hiding,' said James. 'Waiting for us to show ourselves. Let me go first and distract him. You follow quickly. Don't be afraid of hitting me.'

'James . . .'

'I need to know you will fire.'

'I will fire.'

'Good. Then let's do it . . .'

James hurled himself into the room, dived at the bed and rolled off the other side, coming to his feet in a fighting stance.

Mathis followed, sweeping the room with his gun.

There was no sign of Caiboche.

Mathis ran a hand through his hair. He was sweating heavily.

'Where is he?'

'We'll do the same again,' said James, stalking over to the bedroom door.

'*Bien sûr.* I wish I was as brave as you, my friend.'

'I wish I had a gun,' said James.

'Have you ever shot a man?'

'No. Have you?'

'*Non.* But there is always a first time. Let's go.'

Once again James pulled the door open and once again there was no sign of Caiboche.

James walked gingerly into the slaughterhouse. It was worse this time – now that he knew what to expect. He was also aware that these were men who René had known well, had spent many days with, had laughed with, shared meals with . . .

Now they were just broken dummies, their brains smashed out. He felt the bile rise in his throat. Mathis put a hand on his shoulder.

'Come on, James,' he said. 'Caiboche has gone.'

★

'So we cannot trust the crew?' said Mathis as they ran through the ship towards the lounge.

'No,' said James, who had told Mathis all he knew. 'We can't trust anyone.'

'But surely the captain is not involved?'

'No,' said James. 'They wouldn't have needed to smuggle guns on board if that were the case. But the captain and all the senior officers will be at the concert. By the time we find him and get him to listen, Caiboche could have escaped and Wilder could be dead.'

'He will listen to me,' said Mathis.

They were near the lounge now and they slowed down, then stopped altogether to peer cautiously round the last corner.

Dumas was standing outside the door of the lounge on the far side of the concourse, trying to look casual, but he was obviously there to stop anyone else going in. The curtains at the windows were all still drawn.

'They haven't gone anywhere,' James whispered. 'And we have to assume that Wilder's with them.'

'You stay here and keep watch,' said Mathis. 'I will go and alert the captain.'

'We don't have time,' said James. 'They have Wilder.'

'We could rush them.'

'There are too many of them.'

'What do you remember from inside the lounge?' said Mathis. 'Anything that might be of any help?'

'There's a smoking deck at the back,' said James. 'One of us could climb down to it from the promenade deck.'

'I will go,' said Mathis.

'No,' said James. 'You're the only one of us the captain will listen to. Do you have a watch?'

'*Oui.*'

'Be back here, with the captain and anyone else who can help, in ten minutes.'

'Then what?'

'Then start shooting.'

'At what?'

'Anything you like. Dumas, perhaps, he deserves it. Drive him back inside and try to keep the rest of them in there while I get Wilder away via the smoking deck.'

'I don't like it,' said Mathis.

'Neither do I,' said James. 'But I'm not sure we have any choice.'

The rain was coming down heavily, driving across the deck from the north-west. It rattled against the windows and made running difficult. James had his head down and his collar up, pinching it closed at his neck with one hand. He was using his other hand to shield his face. He was hurrying along as fast as he dared, desperately worried about Wilder. If the men had done anything to her he would never forgive himself.

In his haste he almost ran slap bang into more trouble, but managed to skid to a halt and dive into the shadows behind a ventilator cowling.

A crewmember was lying unconscious on the deck and Argente, his long silver hair hanging in rat's tails about his face, was with five of the French 'gymnastics team' who were clumsily attempting to release one of the lifeboats. They were obviously getting ready to leave the *Colombie* and meet up with the *Perceval*. James scanned the ocean. He could see no lights, but, with all this rain, visibility was poor and he had no idea from what direction the other vessel might be approaching.

None of Argente's men appeared to be armed. Neither was James, though, and the 'gymnasts' were huge.

James backtracked, ducked indoors and crossed to the other side of the ship. From there he carefully made his way towards the stern. Aware that time was ticking away.

There was another man keeping watch on this side. A big

burly fellow, who was swigging from a bottle of rum, seemingly oblivious to the rain that dripped off his shaven head. James made a quick decision and trusted to fate. He left his cover and ran full pelt towards the man. At the last moment he threw himself to the deck and slid the last few feet into the startled man's legs, taking them out from under him. He went down like a felled tree and his head clonked against the railing. He was out for the count. He sat on the wet boards, slumped against a capstan, dazed and unmoving.

James stuffed the bottle into the crook of the man's arm and walked on. With any luck, if any of the guard's friends spotted him sitting there they would assume he had simply drunk too much.

James crossed the open decking at the rear of the ship and glanced back to where the other men were still struggling with the lifeboat on the far side. They were too distracted to spot him as he darted from one patch of shadow to another. His luck held and he made it to the taffrail unseen.

He looked over the edge. The curved smoking deck jutted out from the stern of the *Colombie* about fifteen feet below. Beyond it was a long drop down to where the twin propellers churned the ocean into a boiling fury.

Before he climbed over the taffrail James once again checked on Argente and his men. The lifeboat was swinging loose now but the six of them by no means had the situation under control. They were shouting at each other and trying to grab some dangling ropes.

James slithered over the rail and lowered himself down the other side until he was dangling from the steel lip at the edge of the promenade deck, his fingers slipping on the wet metal. He looked down then dropped silently, landing like a cat on the smoking deck.

He instantly threw himself to the floor and made his body as flat as he could, then crabbed his way to the side where he was safely out of sight of anyone indoors. He waited there until he

*JAMES SLITHERED OVER THE RAIL AND LOWERED HIMSELF
DOWN THE OTHER SIDE . . .*

was sure that nobody was going to come out and investigate, then eased himself into a better position to get a look at what was going on inside the lounge.

He let out his breath in a long sigh of relief.

Wilder was all right. She was still sitting on the leather settee, tired and miserable, and for the moment, forgotten. But at least she looked unhurt.

The men in the lounge mostly had their backs to the smoking deck. All eyes were on what was happening inside. There was a sense of hushed tension in the room.

Caiboche was there. Standing at the table where Emil had sat earlier. The empty guns lined up neatly in front of him. Emil himself was slumped in a chair, his injured foot up on another chair, wrapped in a bloody hand towel. It would have taken some strength and courage to pull the knife out. James was reminded that despite his dandyish appearance Emil was a hardened soldier like the rest of them.

Caiboche picked up a rifle.

'You are a fool,' he shouted loud enough for James to hear. 'An imbecile. Bettered by a mere boy.'

His words were evidently aimed at Maury, who sat at another table, his head bowed.

'You are no more use to me than these guns,' said Caiboche and he hurled the rifle at Maury. Maury flinched as the gun struck him hard in the shoulder and fell to the carpet. Three more guns followed, flying across the room and battering the stocky young man. They must have hurt like the devil, but Maury sat there trying not to move or show any pain.

Then Caiboche sat down and became very still again. He carried on talking to Maury in his soft girlish voice. James couldn't make out the words but their meaning was clear. Maury withered under this quiet verbal assault more than he had when the four heavy guns had been thrown at him.

James wanted to hear what was being said, and he was just

moving to press his ear up against a crack in the door when Caiboche came alive again. Quick as a striking snake he was up from his seat and had grabbed Maury by the back of his head.

James turned away as Caiboche smashed Maury face first into the table.

'Imbecile!' he shouted. 'You should know what happens to men who let me down.'

Maury tried to speak but his voice was a gurgle.

Everyone's attention was fully on Caiboche now. They watched him in appalled fascination. The general, his face expressionless, was pressing down on the back of Maury's head. He looked like a manual labourer at work. He was concentrating hard and his arms shook with the effort. Maury struggled, but couldn't break free from the man's iron grip. His feet beat out a fast pattern on the floor. Caiboche continued to exert enormous pressure, forcing Maury's face into the tabletop.

James couldn't watch, and he saw Wilder cover her face with her hands as there came a loud crack and a crunch followed by a gasp.

James wondered if now was the moment to move, while the men were distracted, but he knew that if he opened the door they would all hear it. The sound of the wind and the waves and the engines was very loud out here.

And then he sensed a movement in the salon. Somebody was approaching the doors. He shrank back and folded himself into the shadows under a table.

The doors opened and two of the 'gymnasts' came out carrying Maury, one at either end. Thankfully James couldn't see his face. The men heaved and tossed the lifeless body over the rail into the ocean.

Since he had left James, Mathis had not been idle. He had raced to the dining room, his heart in his mouth. Signor Ponzi was still on stage, acknowledging the cheers and applause of his audience. Mathis had spotted the captain sitting in an upper gallery to the side and had pushed his way through the seats to reach him. He had garbled a message to the old man, and left him standing there in stunned silence as he had hurried back to the lounge.

Mathis was going to do all he could to make sure that James and his friend Wilder got out of this safely. He would not miss the ten-minute deadline.

As he reached his hiding place by the concourse he checked his watch. He had less than a minute to spare.

And then what?

Tick-tick-tick-tick-tick-tick-tick . . .

Cold sweat dripped down his neck. His throat was painfully dry. How he would love a drink now. A brandy, strong and harsh.

Where was the damned captain? Perhaps Mathis should have stayed to make sure his message was understood?

Alors. What's done is done.

He cautiously stuck the muzzle of his pistol round the corner and peered out after it.

Dumas was still there, standing by the door to the lounge. Mathis raised his sights and levelled them at the ship's officer. He looked as uncomfortable and jumpy as Mathis felt.

When it came to it, what would he do? Dumas was working for the butcher who had slaughtered his friends, but could he really shoot him in cold blood?

He looked once again at his watch. The second hand was ticking steadily round towards midnight. He would make the decision then. And not before. As he pulled the trigger his hand would know where to aim.

Tick-tick-tick-tick-tick-tick-tick . . .

James heard Caiboche's voice from inside the salon.

'Men are nothing more than insects to me,' he said.

As if that were a cue, a gunshot sounded.

Mathis.

There was pandemonium in the lounge. Men running around shouting. The sound of a door opening and closing. Dumas's voice.

The two 'gymnasts' ran back inside and James followed in a low crouch.

He took one quick look round the room. Emil had his pistol out and was limping towards Dumas who stood by the door at the far end. The men were all watching him, including Caiboche, who was wiping his hands on a cloth. There was a pool of sticky blood on the table, which had been split almost in two.

James raced over to Wilder and grabbed her hand. Wilder was too stunned by events to know how to react and looked at James as if he was a ghost. Before she could say anything, James hauled her out of her seat and dragged her back the way he had come. They stumbled out into the rain. The sharp air hit Wilder like a slap in the face and the life came back into her eyes.

'Get up there, quick!' James hissed, nodding towards the promenade deck above their heads and making a stirrup of his hands. Wilder did as she was told without question. She stepped into his hands and he hoisted her into the air in one firm, swift movement. She grabbed hold of the slippery metal and as she pulled herself up she swung a leg out to the side. Soon she was scrambling under the rail.

There were shots from inside the lounge. Thankfully not aimed at James, but he needed to get away before anyone realized what was going on. He sprang on to the side rail, hardly aware of the giddy drop down the other side to the seething chilly waters of the Atlantic. Then he jumped up after Wilder and in few seconds he was safely on the promenade deck.

Someone inside the lounge was firing back at him now, but Mathis was keeping his head down. His ears were still ringing from his own shot. Propelled by exploding gases the bullet had torn through the air and clanged into the ironwork inches from Dumas's head.

Dumas had yelled and made a dive for the door. Moving surprisingly fast for a man of his size.

Mathis sighed. In the end his hand hadn't made the final decision. The hand of God had.

He had been aiming for Dumas's head.

Emil was the only one of the rescuers who had a loaded gun. He had brought it on board with him in Venezuela – just in case. He was crouching down by the windows that looked in towards the concourse. He had drawn back a curtain, smashed the glass for a clear shot and fired off three rounds, but there was no sign of their attackers.

'Can you see them?' called Caiboche.

'*Non.* They are hiding like women.'

'How many?'

'I do not know. I saw one for sure. There may be more.'

Caiboche was sitting still as a corpse at a table, staring at the clock on the wall. It was impossible to read what he might be thinking or feeling.

The other men crawled about the carpet cursing and shouting at each other.

'Where is the girl?'

'This is all your fault.'

'We should stop cowering in here and charge them.'

'They will cut us down.'

Insects.

Useless insects.

James lay on the deck, next to the shivering Wilder, one arm round her. They weren't out of danger yet. Argente and the others were still by the lifeboat, which dangled uselessly at an alarming tilt. They had obviously heard the shots and were arguing about what to do. Save themselves or go down to help the *général*?

Their argument was cut short by the noisy arrival of several crewmembers armed with truncheons, who laid into them with merciless professionalism. Argente fought back like a tiger, but he was chopped down in seconds and the five remaining men quickly surrendered.

James jumped up and shouted with joy.

'Looks like the cavalry's arrived at last,' he said.

'We're all right,' said Wilder. 'We're all right.'

She buried her face in James's chest and added her tears to his already soaking shirt.

On the deck below the captain was hurrying along behind four sailors carrying rifles. They spotted Mathis up ahead, squatting on the floor, his back against the wall.

He grinned when he saw the reinforcements.

'Not before time,' he said.

The captain sniffed.

'I never wanted that man on my ship in the first place. I knew he would be nothing but trouble.'

'If your men shoot him,' said Mathis. 'It will save the courts in France a lot of time and money.'

'The owners of this ship would not be pleased to find her shot to pieces,' said the captain. 'I want this over with quickly.'

'Good luck,' said Mathis.

THEIR ARGUMENT WAS CUT SHORT BY THE NOISY ARRIVAL OF
SEVERAL CREWMEMBERS ARMED WITH TRUNCHEONS ...

★

Caiboche had a gun in his belt. He had taken it off a dead gendarme. But what was the use? It was too late to fight his way out now. The crew of the *Colombie* had the upper hand. The element of surprise had been lost.

He tossed the gun to one of his men, a corporal, like a man tossing a scrap of meat to a dog.

'To the death,' he said quietly. The corporal swallowed and nodded, looking at the gun as if it was a scorpion in his hand.

He stood up to fire at the same time as Emil loosed a barrage of shots through the broken window.

In the return fire the corporal was hit in the chest.

Caiboche ordered another man to pick up the fallen gun.

Then they heard the captain's voice.

'Put down your weapons and surrender. There is nowhere you can go!'

The men looked to Caiboche.

'Imbeciles,' he said softly, looked once more at the clock, and then stood up.

'*Capitaine!*' he called. 'I do not intend to return to France in chains. *Adieu!*'

He saluted, turned on his heel and sprinted towards the smoking deck. His men watched in astonishment as he shot out of the doors like a bullet, vaulted over the rail and launched himself soundlessly into the empty night.

Three of them ran after him, but by the time they got to the rail Caiboche had disappeared into the foaming sea behind the ship.

They stood there dumbfounded.

Their general was gone.

Emil realized that their position was hopeless. With no Caiboche there was nothing to fight for. He tossed his gun out through the broken window.

★

The rain had stopped and James was standing at the taffrail with Wilder. They knew that soon there would be questions and explanations and more excitement, so they were relishing their last few minutes of calm together before the storm hit.

The ship's crew had rounded up the last of Caiboche's men and Mathis was being hailed as the hero of the day. The young gendarme had done well. James hoped he'd get his promotion for this, and his transfer to Paris. James had had a quiet word with him and asked him to play down his own role in what had happened. He didn't want the attention. He had been hoping to return to a normal life back in England, but trouble seemed to follow him around like a sick dog.

The captain was also hoping to play matters down so as not to alarm the other passengers and destroy the reputation of the shipping line who paid his wages.

Wilder put her hand on James's.

'Is it really over?' she said.

'Yes.'

They stared out at the ship's wake: a faint trail of paler grey against the rolling darkness of the ocean.

'Is he dead, do you suppose?' Wilder asked.

'If he didn't die when he hit the water . . . If he wasn't sucked under by turbulence . . . How long could he survive out there?'

'What happened to the boat that was meant to pick him up?'

'Who knows?' said James. 'Maybe his men were meant to send a signal or something . . . but whatever happened it never showed up. If Caiboche *is* alive now he'll drown soon enough, or freeze to death, or be eaten by sharks. Good riddance, I say. People talk about evil. I don't suppose many men can be called that, not *truly* evil . . . But he was one of them.'

Wilder shivered and James hugged her tight.

'Don't worry,' he said. 'You'll never see him again . . .'

★

Caiboche was floating in the water. His pale square head just showing above the swell, his legs working hard to keep him stable. How long could he keep this up for? He had broken an arm when he hit the water, and had blacked out for a few seconds. He had woken in a world of cold, black death, but had fought his way to the surface and was still alive. He would keep himself alive by the sheer force of his will. His body was growing numb, though; his temperature lowering degree by degree. Unconsciousness would soon return if he did not fight it.

He had survived many ordeals before. On the streets of Marseilles when he had been nearly beaten to death by a rival gang. In the harsh police cells. In Africa with the Legion. In the living hell of the trenches in the Great War. The attack on Aziz . . .

He would survive this. It wasn't over yet.

He knew he couldn't swim anywhere, though. It was thousands of miles to the nearest land.

Never mind. If he could just keep afloat there was still a chance. He was a hard man to kill.

Already the *Colombie* was disappearing. Her shape, made up of myriad twinkling lights, growing smaller and smaller as she steamed steadily onwards.

Just before he had jumped he had checked the clock. Ten thirty. The exact time of the intended pick-up. The captain of the *Perceval* would have calculated the position of the *Colombie*. Would have been following and tracking her for the last few hundred kilometres. But how accurate was her equipment? Caiboche was not a naval man. He didn't know about these things.

And where was she?

The *Perceval* should have been here by now.

If he could just hang on to life for a minute longer, five minutes, ten . . .

And then he felt it. Vibrations pulsing through the water.

Something huge rising from the depths. Finally the throb of engines.

In a moment, not a hundred metres from where he swam, he saw a conning tower break the surface.

He allowed himself a small smile of triumph.

The submarine had arrived.

He watched as a tiny figure appeared atop the tower and called across the water with a loud hailer.

'*Ici!*' cried Caiboche. 'I am here!'

'Nobody can hold a Bond forever ...'

James Bond

Appearance: Tall for his age, slim, with dark hair and grey-blue eyes.

Distinguishing features: An unruly comma-shaped lock of hair that constantly falls on to his forehead. In Scotland, James is viciously attacked by Lord Hellebore with a riding crop – if you look closely, you can still see the scar on James's cheek.

Background: Born in Zurich, raised in both London and Switzerland from the age of six. An only child, James is also an orphan – his parents died when he was just eleven.

Skills: Speaks fluent English, French and German. A naturally talented runner who excels at most sports; can also box. Can drive but is not yet old enough to obtain a licence.

Personal qualities: Very intelligent and quietly confident. Enjoys his own company but can make friends easily if he wants to. Hates feeling trapped and has even worked out a night-time 'escape route' from his room at Eton. Has an adventurous streak and will take risks if necessary.

Likes: His aunt, uncle and close friends, the Bamford and Martin motor car, Bentley Blowers, good food. Loves the feeling of freedom that he gets from running. Enjoys driving for similar reasons.

Dislikes: Studying Latin, Codrose's cooking, bullies of any kind, cheats, the Eton school uniform, disloyalty.

Ambitions: To be an explorer and see more of the world. Or perhaps follow in his uncle's footsteps and become a spy.

Living in two different countries always seemed normal to James. He was brought up by his Swiss mother, Monique, but saw much less of his father, Andrew, who was often away working. Mr Bond's restless personality meant he was forever on the move, visiting new places and travelling. He loved sports such as riding, skiing and sailing, and his wife accompanied him on frequent holidays abroad. James grew used to his parents being away. He would stay with family members, often visiting his favourite relative, Aunt Charmian, at her cottage in Kent.

It was during one of these stays that James and his aunt received the devastating news. His parents had been killed in a climbing accident in the French Alps.

'James was alone in the world now, and he would have to make it on his own.'

July 1933   **ETON COLLEGE**

Dear Miss Bond,

James Bond – Report on Attendance, Conduct and Progress

As James's Classical Tutor, I am pleased to see that he
has settled in well to the school, despite starting one
half later than the other boys. His general conduct is
good and his attendance record so far, excellent.

James is clearly an intelligent and personable boy who
displays a lively and enquiring mind. He has shown
promise in many subjects, particularly in the area of
Modern Languages, though he must not allow his natural
linguistic ability to be an excuse for complacence.
I do feel, however, that James could excel further
academically if he could only put his mind to it. He
really must make more effort in Classical Studies,
despite his obvious reluctance to master Latin and Greek.

As regards Games, I am pleased to say that James appears
to be a natural athlete. He competed in the Hellebore
Cup this year and took first place in the cross-country
section, for which he is to be commended. However, James
shows less enthusiasm for team sports, which is a loss
for both himself and the school.

Generally speaking, James has made a promising start
to his school career and I feel sure that I will be
overseeing his time here with great interest.

Yours sincerely,

Michael Merriot

Mr Michael Merriot

Charmian Bond

Appearance: Tall, dark-haired and grey-eyed.

Personality: Confident, clever and opinionated; also warm and caring.

Location: The village of Pett Bottom in Kent. Often away travelling around the world.

Skills: Drives extremely fast, speaks five languages and is very well-read.

'You didn't often see a woman in trousers, but Charmian carried herself so confidently that nobody would have dared to criticize her.'

Charmian and James may be related, but first and foremost they are great friends. They have a lot in common: intelligence, a great sense of adventure, strong personalities and a love of discovering new things. Since James's parents died, his aunt has been a central figure in his life, providing him with the security he needs, while allowing him plenty of freedom.

'We're going to have to look after each other from now on, you and I.'

James is very fond of his aunt and he always looks forward to visiting her. He especially enjoys being driven in her magnificent Bentley Blower, which, given Charmian's taste for speed, is always an experience.

Charmian treats James as an equal and involves him in many aspects of her exciting life as a globe-trotting anthropologist. An ideal job for Charmian, it allows her to indulge her fascination with peoples and cultures in different lands.

LIFE AS AN ANTHROPOLOGIST

Anthropology is about people: where they come from, and how they live. Anthropologists such as Charmian study different peoples by travelling around the world and living with them, sometimes for years. Charmian has shared the lives of people in all corners of the globe, from Eskimos in icy Greenland to the Paduang hill-tribes of Burma (who stretch their necks to amazing lengths with brass rings). She loves her work and finds it endlessly fascinating.

The hidden tribe of Mexico

Charmian embarks on an exciting expedition into the Mexican rainforest in search of a mysterious tribe – one believed never to have seen an outsider before. As always, she takes her trusty leather saddlebag, containing vital equipment such as a first–aid kit, compass, water bottle and maps.

Deep in the Mexican rainforest live a tribe of Mayan Indians called the Lacandones. They are believed to be descendants of the ancient Mayans, a civilisation whose origins go back to 1500 BC. The ancient Mayans once lived in warring city states and were renowned for their architecture, building temples for religious worship and sacrifice.

During the sixteenth century the Lacandon Mayans fled from the Spanish Conquistadores into the rainforest in Chiapas, Mexico's southernmost state. Here, they survived, undiscovered for hundreds of years, until the early twentieth century. Anthropologists were fascinated to find that the Lacandones had kept many of their ancient ways, living off the land and hunting deer and monkeys with bows and arrows. They also worshipped 'heavenly gods' that dwelt in the sky and 'earthly gods' who lived underground. Another ritual still being practised by the tribe until the late nineteenth century, was the ancient Mayan art of headshaping.

MAYAN HEADSHAPING

Children aged one to three would have their heads strapped between two wooden boards and wrapped tightly in cloth. This compressed the head from back to front, and slowly flattened it, changing the shape of their head over time.

The ancient Mayans thought this was important because, to them, the shape of the head represented one's status in society – flattened heads shaped like cones indicated good family heritage. They also believed that the wrapping supplied a roof over the child's head, protecting them from evil spirits.

Max Bond

Appearance: Tall, lean and dapper. Has a limp caused by a wartime injury, when he broke his leg escaping from German interrogators. Hiding out in the woods, it never healed properly.

Personality: Friendly, charming, capable and very intelligent.

Location: The West Highland village of Keithly.

Skills: An ex-army captain turned spy, Max can turn his hand to most things. He is a skilled artist, speaks fluent German, and is an excellent driver.

 *'A lot of what I did in the war was secret.'*

Uncle Max – his life

Uncle Max is a hugely influential person in James's life. He cut a dashing figure when James was younger, turning up to take his nephew out on exciting day trips. Years later, James is shocked to see his dying uncle's appearance. Hollow-eyed, gaunt and racked by fits of coughing, Max knows that his days are numbered. But he still has a huge zest for life, and can't wait to teach James about two of his great loves: fishing and driving.

Max reveals a surprising side of his personality to James. Recalling his memories of the First World War, he tells James a secret never before revealed to anyone – that he was once a spy.

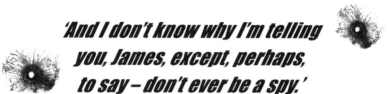

'And I don't know why I'm telling you, James, except, perhaps, to say – don't ever be a spy.'

James is given a glimpse of another world, a world of confidential briefings, forged papers and secret training, involving passwords, poisons and unarmed combat.

Max was recruited as an agent while fighting in the First World War. Hit by a bullet and hospitalized, he got talking to a man who told him that British Intelligence were looking for fluent speakers of German. Max underwent training to become an undercover agent and was later smuggled by boat into German territory, where he lived under a false identity. He was now Herr Grumann, an ordinary German railway engineer.

ABOUT BRITISH INTELLIGENCE

'Information is the most
important weapon in
your arsenal.'

The Foreign Section of the Secret Service
Bureau operated a network of agents who
worked in German territory before and during
the First World War. The intelligence they
gained made a crucial contribution to the
Allied victory.

THE HISTORY OF THE BUREAU

The Secret Service Bureau was created in 1909 at a
time when Britain faced an increasing threat from
Germany. At that time, Germany and Britain were
rivals in a naval arms race, with both countries
desperate to gain superiority for their fleets. German
spies were known to be operating in the UK, and
British naval ports were in danger. It was decided
that an organization must be set up to deal with the
threat.

The Secret Service Bureau had two aims:

- To counter foreign espionage in the UK. The Home
  Section dealt with this. The **Home Section** later
  became the **Security Service** – now known as **Military
  Intelligence 5** or **MI5**.

- To collect intelligence from abroad – covered by
  the Foreign Section. Around 1920, the **Foreign
  Section** became the **Secret Intelligence Service**,
  or SIS for short. It is still known as the **SIS**
  today but is more often referred to as **Military
  Intelligence 6** or **MI6**.

After the First World War, the Secret Service
Bureau continued its work, and its focus was
now also on Russian espionage and the threat
of international communism. Germany was still
a priority for the Bureau, though, as the Nazi
party was gaining in strength and power. Up until
the start of the Second World War in 1939 it was
essential for the Foreign Section – the SIS –
to find out more about German plans and military
capabilities.

CAPTAIN MANSFIELD CUMMING

The first head of the Foreign Section was Captain
Sir Mansfield Cumming RN, who oversaw all its work
in the First World War. By January 1918 he had more
than 400 agents reporting to him on German troop
movements in occupied Belgium and northern France.

Cumming always signed himself simply as 'MC' or
'C' in green, so beginning a tradition whereby all
future Section heads would be known as 'C' and sign
their documents using green ink.

By all accounts, Cumming was a colourful character.
He had a wooden leg, having lost his limb in a car
accident. According to one of his stories, he was
forced to cut his own leg off with a penknife to
escape the wreck. Often, to get his point across
– or simply to shock – he would stab a paper-knife
into his leg while he was speaking. Those not in
the know about his accident would be horrified to
see it sticking out of his leg, while Cumming
carried on with the conversation unperturbed.

Cumming loved spy disguises and gadgets, and often experimented with them. He was also known for driving his Rolls-Royce extremely fast around London.

One of the spies Cumming personally recruited was a man called Sidney Reilly, who went on to become one of Britain's most important secret agents.

REILLY - ACE OF SPIES

Sidney Reilly was a cover name - Reilly was, in fact, born Georgi Rosenblum in Russia in 1874. A clever, charismatic man who could speak seven languages, Reilly enjoyed an extravagant lifestyle and loved women, travelling, gambling and fine food. Because of these high-class tastes he was nicknamed the 'gentleman spy'.

Reilly was a master of disguise. During his spying career he successfully posed as a Russian arms merchant, a German officer and even a Catholic priest. On one mission, he was sent to Germany to get information about their new weapons. Reilly disguised himself as an German shipyard worker and found the weapon plans, but was caught in the act by the shipyard foreman. Reilly strangled him and made his escape.

In 1925 Reilly was captured by the Russians during a secret mission. Throughout his imprisonment he kept tiny notes about their interrogation techniques, written on cigarette papers and hidden in the plaster wall, in case the information might be useful to the SIS one day. But Reilly never got home. He was shot by the Russians and his body buried in the grounds of Lubyanka Prison.

SOME SPY TERMINOLOGY

Agents and their contacts operate using words and terms that are unique to the business of spying.

- AGENT: A person able to provide secret reporting on a target of investigation.

- AGENT-IN-PLACE: A person who remains in his or her ordinary job but is actually in that job to get secret information.

- AGENT PROVOCATEUR: An undercover agent who becomes friendly with a target. Their aim is to get that person to unknowingly incriminate themselves.

- BLACK OPERATION: An operation that has not been authorized by the head organization.

- COVER: A secret agent needs a 'cover' – a fictitious name and other personal details to make their behaviour seem convincing.

- BLOWN: When an agent has been found out ('My cover has been blown').

- COMPROMISED: An agent who is 'compromised' has been discovered and can no longer do the job.

- DEAD DROP: A secret location in which sensitive materials or documents are left for a contact to collect.

- DEFECTOR: A person who is no longer loyal to their original country. Defectors usually flee abroad, though some may stay where they are and become double agents.

- DOUBLE AGENT: A spy who pretends to work for one country while actually working as a spy for another.

- RABBIT: The person under investigation, also known as the target of the operation.

- ROLLED UP: An operation that ends with an agent's arrest.

- SAFE HOUSE: A secret location known only to agents, and therefore a place of refuge.

Uncle Max's cover is blown while he is in Germany. One night a group of German soldiers arrives to take him away for interrogation, an ordeal from which he never fully recovers.

MI5 AND MI6 TODAY

MI5 is the security intelligence agency for the UK. Based in London, it is responsible for protecting the country against threats to national security, including terrorism and espionage. The SIS, or MI6, operates worldwide to collect secret foreign intelligence. It promotes and defends the security of the UK and mounts covert operations overseas. To do this, it liaises with many other foreign intelligence and security services, such as the CIA in the United States, as well as with the Ministry of Defence and the Foreign and Commonwealth Office.

Agents are also known as 'covert human intelligence sources' and they are still a vital source of information today. Operations, some of which can continue for years, are run by specially trained officers at HQ. Other ways of gaining sensitive information are through surveillance and intercepting communications. These days, all kinds of advanced technology can be used to help agents watch targets. Spy gadgets include electronic eavesdropping devices that can 'hear' conversations through thick walls and advanced thermal-imaging cameras, which can detect the heat of a hidden human being – even in darkness and smoke. These cameras can also tell agents if a car has been recently moved, by showing the heat marks left in the road by the vehicle's tyres.

Modern-day agents are often recruited through advertisements in the newspaper or on the MI5 and MI6 websites. One such advert announced that the agencies were looking for people who were 'not afraid to take well-calculated decisions under pressure'. This is a far cry from the days of Uncle Max, who was quietly put in touch with the intelligence services by a contact who was 'in the know'. Many secret agents in the past were recruited in this way, as the intelligence services often sent out 'scouts' to find suitable candidates at top universities, like Oxford and Cambridge.

The time that Uncle Max and James spend together in Scotland is precious to both of them. As they talk, walk and fish, Max tells James things he has never revealed to anyone else — and James learns a great deal from his uncle's wise words and tales of past experiences. And when James is in the most danger, it is the voice of Uncle Max that will pull him through.

'Nobody can hold a Bond forever...'

Eton *Life*

'The smell and the noise and confusion
of a hallway full of schoolboys can be quite awful
at twenty past seven in the morning.'

When James first arrives at Eton College at Easter, 1933, he finds it a bewildering and unsettling place. Governed by strict rules and ancient traditions, there is a huge amount of information for a new pupil to take in. Luckily, James is a fast learner. He soon settles in and begins to make friends – and also a few enemies.

The school has traditions that go back hundreds of years, some of which may seem strange to an outsider. Not even the Eton boys themselves are sure why many of these rules exist. As Pritpal remarks:

> ### 'Nobody knows why we do most of the things we do.'

But, as James finds out, it is vital to learn about the ways of the school, not least because he will soon have to sit a Colours Test – an exam that all new boys must take to check their knowledge of the school.

SOME ETON SCHOOL RULES

- Umbrellas must be carried unrolled
- Boys must not be seen chewing in the street
- Never turn down the collar of your coat
- Junior boys must only walk on the east side of the High Street
- Tickets (slips of paper) must be obtained if you wish to leave your House out-of-hours
- A white or a yellow ticket will be given to boys who have done wrong. The yellow tickets are the most feared - they are only given to boys who have committed serious offences

> ### 'James hated rules.'

About the School

Eton College is Britain's most famous public school, and also one of the oldest, having been founded by King Henry VI in 1440. It is a large boys' school, which today has 1,300 pupils. Many famous and powerful men have been educated at Eton over the years, including 19 prime ministers, several members of the Royal Family, the poet Shelley, and writers George Orwell, and Peter and Ian Fleming.

The school is in Eton, just a few minutes' walk across the river from Windsor, a town famous for the magnificent Windsor Castle. This is the largest and oldest occupied castle in the world, and an important residence for the Royal Family. Windsor is a picturesque place, located on the banks of the River Thames, about 30 kilometres outside London.

Like James, all of the boys are boarders who live in the school's numerous Houses scattered around the town.

SPOTTISWOODE'S

The traditional bookshop in the High Street where every Eton boy purchased his school books. (It was closed after the Second World War.)

LONG WALK

A wide pedestria area lined with li trees, adjacent to College Building

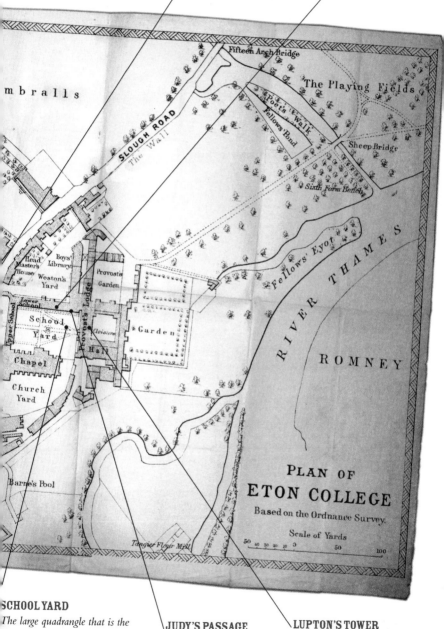

THE BURNING BUSH

A famous Eton meeting point. It is not a plant but a wrought-iron lamp, which once stood on its own little island in the middle of the Windsor–Slough road. It has since been moved off the road, and is situated outside the School Library.

COLLEGE

The original school building, built in 1443. This is where the teachers live. When James was at Eton they were often called 'masters'.

PLAN OF
ETON COLLEGE
Based on the Ordnance Survey.

Scale of Yards

SCHOOL YARD

The large quadrangle that is the hub of the school. This is also where College Chapel is located.

JUDY'S PASSAGE

A short cut through the centre of the school.

LUPTON'S TOWER

The Tudor clock tower at the far end of School Yard.

Accommodation

In the 1930s, every Eton boy was given his own room, furnished with a burry (a kind of desk), a washstand, a chair and a rug. They used this room for studying, socializing and for eating many of their meals.

James's room is tiny, with a sloping roof; his new friend, Pritpal, is next door. The boys have fireplaces in their rooms but are allowed only one large lump of coal every other day. On cold days, the rooms are freezing, cold enough for the boys to wear gloves.

TIMETABLE

Time	Subject	Comment
.00 a.m.		Boys are woken by the maid, who rings a loud handbell.
.30 a.m.	Early School	The first lesson of the day.
.15 a.m.	Breakfast at boys' Houses	(Codrose's for James)
.00 a.m.	Private study in rooms	
45 a.m.	Chapel	
.15 a.m.	Second School	
.00 a.m.	Chambers	A daily meeting for masters, and a refreshment for the boys, sometimes hot chocolate and buns
.30 a.m.	Third School	
.15 p.m.	Pupil Room for junior boys	This time is spent doing Latin or Greek with their tutors.
15 p.m.	Boys' dinner	
15 p.m.	Sport	For junior boys, the Field Game in the winter, and usually cricket or rowing in the summer.
15 p.m.	Fourth School	
00 p.m.	Tea	Boys cook their own tea — this is called 'messing'.
50 p.m.	Fifth School	
5 p.m.	Private Business with tutor	Twice a week
5 p.m.	Supper	
5 p.m.	Society meetings or E.W. (Extra Work)	
00 p.m.	Bedtime	

27763. — Socec.

The boys are responsible for cooking their own tea, a tradition called 'messing'. 'Messmates' from the same House are allocated to each other, and are a small group who cook together and take turns to eat in each other's rooms (James's messmates are Pritpal and Tommy Chong). In their House there is a little electric stove outside the rooms in the passage for cooking foods like eggs and sausages. The Housemaster prepares a hot lunch but, unluckily for James and his friends, Codrose is renowned for his appalling cooking – tough old meat and cold, watery soup. All his boys are forced to buy extra food from the local shops or hope that their families send them a parcel of tasty 'sock'. Snacks can also be bought from the school 'sock shop' (tuck shop).

In the 1930s a group of boys created their own much more delicious dish – the celebrated 'Eton Mess'. This was a sweet dessert made from strawberries or bananas mixed with ice cream or cream. Stirring it all together made the 'mess'. Nowadays, Eton Mess also contains pieces of meringue and it is traditional to eat it on the special holiday of the 'Fourth of June'.

The Importance of Latin

James must spend hours every week studying Classics – Latin, Greek and Ancient History. Latin is his most hated subject – he finds the ancient language incredibly dull (much to the horror of Latin fanatic Mr Cooper-ffrench). But a working knowledge of Latin comes in useful to James on at least one occasion. Returning from the Danger Society one night, he overhears two shadowy strangers discussing *navis* and *sanguis*. He understands that they are talking about 'a boat' and 'blood', and his suspicions are aroused.

LATIN PHRASES

* Carpe diem – seize the day
* Dictum meum pactum – my word is my bond
* Dura lex, sed lex – the law is harsh but it is the law
* Mens rea – guilty mind
* Nihil obstat – nothing stands in the way
* Velle est posse – where there's a will, there's a way

LATIN MOTTOES

* Eton's school motto is Floreat Etona, which means 'May Eton flourish'. Many other organizations have Latin mottoes with special meanings.
* James's family, the Bonds, have their own motto – Orbis non sufficit – which means 'The world is not enough'.
* Per ardua ad astra ('Through adversity to the stars') – the Royal Air Force
* Regnum defende ('Defend the realm') – MI5
* Estote parati ('Be prepared') – the Boy Scouts

THE GLORIOUS FOURTH OF JUNE

The Fourth of June is one of the most important days in the Eton calendar. The school is open to everyone and many families visit to enjoy the rowing events on the Thames, hear the speeches and watch the cricket matches. James is delighted to see his Aunt Charmian arrive to join in the festivities.

The Fourth of June is a holiday in celebration of the birthday of King George III. The king (1760–1820) loved the school and was a great patron of Eton during his reign. He spent much of his time at Windsor Castle and often attended school functions, getting to know the masters and the boys.

The highlight of a full day of celebrations is the traditional Procession of Boats. The best rowers in the school get dressed up in nineteenth-century naval uniform and row past in vintage wooden boats. As they pass the parents assembled on the bank, they salute them by raising their oars and standing up. Very occasionally a boat capsizes, much to the amusement of their audience.

The Fourth of June is the only day of the year when all Eton boys are allowed to carry rolled umbrellas.

The Boys

It isn't long before James makes friends. His pals are a mixed bunch, but all possess the single most important quality for James – absolute loyalty.

Pritpal Nandra

'I have been in England too long.'

Background: Son of an Indian Maharajah.

Personality: Clever and a great mathematician. Rather unadventurous in other ways and distinctly unsporty.

Distinctive features: Pritpal prefers a quiet studious life and doesn't like taking risks. He loves his food and finds the dull cuisine at Eton very hard to cope with. Pritpal is one of James's messmates. He enjoys puzzles, especially crosswords.

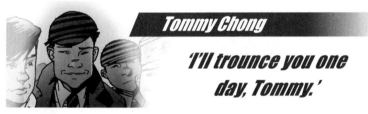

Tommy Chong

'I'll trounce you one day, Tommy.'

Background: Comes from Hong Kong.

Personality: Small, tough and argumentative.

Distinctive features: James's other messmate, Tommy, is the reigning expert when it comes to card games and gambling. Everyone knows that he is practically impossible to beat. Tommy can be rather excitable during a tense game and, for a Chinese boy, knows an awful lot of English swear words.

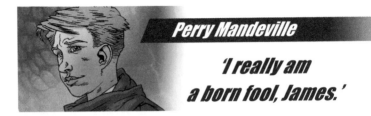

Perry Mandeville

'I really am a born fool, James.'

Background: From a wealthy and aristocratic English family.

Personality: The ultimate thrill-seeker. Restless, can never sit still.

Distinctive features: As the founder of the Danger Society, Perry is often to be found on reckless escapades. He envies James his Bamford and Martin motor car and is always desperate to drive it. Perry has a distinct stammer, mainly because his voice can't keep up with the speed of his thoughts.

Andrew Carlton

'... a hero of the school rowing team ...'

Background: His father was a champion rower.

Personality: Quiet and good-natured, modest about his sporting abilities.

Distinctive features: Andrew is a champion wet bob and a great athlete. Two years older than James, he recruits him to the Danger Society. Andrew beats George Hellebore to the Hellebore Cup and is an excellent marksman.

There are many clubs and societies at Eton. James is a member of just one:

'A secret society dedicated to danger, risk-taking and generally breaking the law of the land.'

HE DANGER SOCIETY

The Danger Society is a secret group of boys who enjoy adventure and taking risks. Perry is the founder and captain of the society. Another member is Mark Goodenough — brother of Amy, one of the girls that James meets on his adventures. James becomes a popular member, being the only one of the group who owns a car, garaged in nearby Windsor.

The Danger Society meets once a week — they are careful not to have a fixed night, to lessen the risk of getting caught. They talk, smoke and make outlandish plans. They know if they are discovered they would all be severely punished — but that just adds to the excitement.

One of Perry's more ludicrous exploits was kidnapping five sheep from a nearby field and shepherding them back to the Head Master's room. He was discovered and, unsurprisingly, got into serious trouble.

For James, the route to the Danger Society HQ is probably the riskiest part of his involvement. Because the outside doors of his House are locked at night – and because the eagle-eyed Codrose stalks the corridors – James must wait till dark, creep out of his room and make his way to a locked storage room by wriggling under the floorboards of the lavatory stalls. Climbing out of the storage room window, he must then traverse several dark roofs, walk along a gutter, and jump over a narrow alleyway. Finally, he arrives at their designated meeting place.

**Danger Society
Intruder Alert**

James employed a clever tactic when first scouting his route to check if anyone ever opened the door of the locked storage room. He fixed a hair across the keyhole and stuck it into place with two tiny dabs of grease. Two weeks later the hair was still there so James knew it was safe. There are a few other ways of doing this.

☠ Gently stick a piece of clear tape from the very bottom of the door to the floor. If the tape is broken on your return, you have your answer.

☠ As you are closing the door to leave, put your hand through the crack and drop a sock directly behind the door. If you get home to find the sock has been pushed away from the back of the door, you'll know someone has been inside.

☠ A similar tactic to the above, but much more messy, is to place an eggcup full of ink behind the door as you leave. A stained carpet will be evidence – not one to try at home.

The only other society that James becomes involved with during his time at Eton is the Crossword Society. The antithesis of the Danger Society, its members prefer to test their intellectual abilities rather than run perilous risks.

The Crossword Society

The club is run by Pritpal, who loves puzzles of all kinds. He is helped by a very clever teacher called Mr Fairburn, who devises cryptic crossword puzzles for *The Times* as a hobby. The members meet every Thursday evening in a back room of Spottiswoode's. They occasionally have visitors to give talks, among them a strange character called Gordius who purports to be a crossword compiler.

While not exactly James's idea of fun, the activities of the Crossword Society are brought to his attention when Mr Fairburn disappears and sends the Society a strangely worded letter. From then on, Pritpal's puzzle-solving skills come in very useful indeed.

THE TIMES CRYPTIC CROSSWORD

The Times *newspaper is famous for its cryptic crossword, a particular type of crossword that needs to be solved through careful thinking.*

● *What the clue appears to say when read normally may have nothing to do with the actual answer. The reader must try to find the clues beneath the surface, a bit like cracking a code.*

● *When Pritpal explains the clue 'top-secret monkey' to James, he tells him the answer is 'apex'. Ape means monkey, and if the monkey were a secret agent he might be called Agent X. So a 'top-secret monkey' is Ape X.*

The cryptic crossword in The Times *has always been known for its difficulty and is enjoyed by puzzle-solvers who like a challenge. The people who create the puzzles – called 'setters' or 'compilers' – usually give themselves a name that hides their identity – a pseudonym. Mr Fairburn's pseudonym is 'Deadlock', and* The Times *compiler who visits the Society is 'Gordius'. Some well-known modern-day compilers are 'Araucaria', 'Poncho' and 'Himmler'.*

The first British crosswords appeared in newspapers in the 1920s and one early crossword setter was called 'Torquemada'. He was famous for very difficult cryptic puzzles. (The original Torquemada was the head of the Spanish Inquisition, which was infamous for its use of torture.)

● *A former crossword editor of* The Times, *Edmund Akenhead, has a favourite clue. The answer has seven blank spaces, but there is no clue given at all. Can you guess the seven-letter word?*

● *Torquemada, the master of tricky cryptic clues, would sometimes deliberately use misspellings. Here is one example: 'What makes dat guy's appearance that guy's?'*

1. Missing.   2. Disguise

SOME ETON VOCABULARY

Boys often use special Eton words, which are unique to the college. Like the school traditions, these words have been used for hundreds of years.

Abracadabra – the academic timetable

Bill – if a boy misbehaves he is placed 'on the bill' and seen by the Head Master or Lower Master for an appropriate punishment

Burry – a combination of a desk, chest of drawers and a small bookcase. Eton boys have one in their rooms.

Dry bob – a boy who plays cricket

E.W. – Extra Work, usually refers to Prep or Homework

Half – the Eton word for 'term'. The school year used to be split into two halves, and the name remained after it was changed to three terms.

Mesopotamia, Dutchman's, Agar's Plough – the various Eton playing fields

Pop – a select group of prefects

Rip – if a boy has done a really poor piece of work he may be given a 'rip', i.e. he has to have the work signed by his Housemaster

Show-up – if a boy does a very good piece of work he may get a 'show-up', and also have his work signed by his Housemaster

Slack bob – a boy who does not row or play cricket (Pritpal would probably qualify as this)

Sock – as a verb it means to give someone a tasty treat, e.g. 'I'll sock you an ice cream'. As a noun it simply means food. Sweets are known as 'lush'.

Tardy book – boys who are late must sign the tardy book before breakfast

Wet bob – a boy who is a rower, e.g. Andrew Carlton

POP

James notices small groups of older boys strutting about in brightly coloured waistcoats, keeping the younger ones in order. This is the exclusive group known as 'Pop'.

The proper name of 'Pop' is 'The Eton Society', one of the oldest societies at the school. The name comes from an old cookshop called 'popina', where their meetings were originally held. Members of Pop can wear checked trousers and a fancy waistcoat of their choice. They can carry their umbrellas rolled and sit on the wall on the Long Walk. Until 1960 they carried canes and could hand out beatings without any authorization from a Housemaster. Pop was once a select group, as only existing members were allowed to select new ones. This is no longer the case.

'B-o-o-o-o-o-y!'

The cry of 'Boy' is known as a 'boy call'. James quickly learns that when he hears the dreaded shout, he must drop everything and rush upstairs to do a chore for an older boy. This is the practice known as 'fagging'. At one time, fagging was common in many public schools. The 'fags', or younger boys, would have to do menial tasks for their 'fag-master', such as making his bed, bringing in coal for the fire and taking messages. If a fag was lucky, he might be allotted a considerate fag-master. However, some of the older boys treated their fags badly. In 1832, at Eton, a boy was tossed in a blanket so hard that he nearly died. Other reports say that fags were hauled from their beds by cords fastened to their toes, and used as 'living footballs' by their bullying fag-masters. Fagging was abolished at Eton in 1978.

The Beaks

All teachers (called 'masters') are known to the boys as 'beaks'.

Mr Merriot

'Are you ready to be put through your paces, Bond?'

Job: Classical tutor, in charge of supervising James's education. Also in charge of school athletics. Mr Merriot has always been a teacher, but his wide experience and knowledge of the world indicate that he has not necessarily revealed everything about his past – and present – life.

Appearance: Tall and thin, like a big stick insect, with untidy hair and a large beaky nose. Often has an unlit pipe in his mouth.

Other features: James is fond of Mr Merriot and he is a very influential figure in James's life. Kind and friendly with an easygoing personality, Mr Merriot enthuses about his favourite subjects – Latin and athletics – and encourages James in both (though James much prefers the latter.) Merriot once represented Great Britain at the Olympics, where he won a bronze medal for running the mile. He can now see James's potential as an athlete. Ever supportive of James, Mr Merriot keeps in touch with letters and school work when James is away. He is a mentor and a friend.

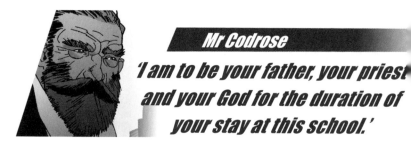

Mr Codrose

'I am to be your father, your priest and your God for the duration of your stay at this school.'

Job: Housemaster. Mr Codrose runs James's House.

Appearance: Thin and pale with a black beard. Has a cold-eyed stare and a self-important air.

Other features: Codrose rules the House with iron discipline. Incredibly suspicious, he patrols the corridors night and day. He is also a stickler for ridiculous rules, such as forcing the boys to keep their pyjamas buttoned to the neck on hot summer nights. These traits make him very unpopular with the boys.

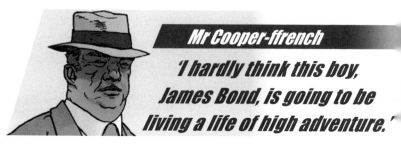

Mr Cooper-ffrench

'I hardly think this boy, James Bond, is going to be living a life of high adventure.'

Job: Tutor and President of the Latin Society

Appearance: A stocky, fierce-looking man with a ruddy complexion and a dapper little moustache. Has no sense of humour.

Other features: Mr Cooper-ffrench is obsessed by the study of Latin and takes offence if others don't agree with his opinions. James's Aunt Charmian is not impressed by his rather patronizing and overexcitable manner. But at heart Cooper-ffrench genuinely cares about the boys and their welfare. As a keen amateur archaeologist, he accompanies Mr Haight and the boys on the school trip to Sardinia.

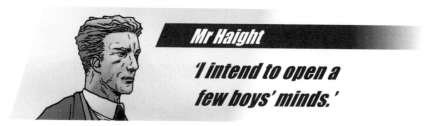

Mr Haight

'I intend to open a few boys' minds.'

Job: History tutor

Appearance: Slightly younger than the other masters, with a kind open face and an athletic build.

Other features: Known to the boys as 'Love-Haight', Peter Haight leads a group of boys on a summer trip to Sardinia with the aim of learning more about the island's historic monuments. But like the ancient Romans he so admires, Haight is tougher than he seems.

Mr Fairburn

'Intelligence is power, James.'

Job: Mathematics tutor. Helps Pritpal run the Crossword Society.

Appearance: Pale with a large nose and ears, and a keen, intelligent expression.

Other features: Though he has a reputation for being eccentric and absent-minded, Alexis Fairburn is a highly intelligent mathematician, who once studied at Cambridge. He loves codes, puzzles and mathematical problems. Fairburn stays in touch with some of his colleagues from Cambridge but they ultimately involve him in something bigger than he can handle. Although he appears English, Fairburn is of Russian parentage. His mother and father disappeared under Lenin's regime and he has never wanted to return to Russia since.

THRASHINGS

The white and yellow tickets doled out by the masters could earn boys punishments ranging from a telling-off to 100 lines of Latin or, at worst, a severe beating. James gets a terrible thrashing from 'Bloody' Bentinck, House Captain of Codrose's, for the crime of being seen with a maid outside school.

'Then there was a grunt, a quick swish, and the cane lashed into his backside with a loud thwack that filled the room.'

In James's time, beatings with canes were executed by the Head Master, Housemaster, Captain of the House or a member of Pop. If a boy was beaten very hard, he might suffer bruising or open, bleeding wounds. These canings were abolished in 1978.

Back in the nineteenth century the punishment was even worse – flogging with a birch rod. This was a very painful and undignified punishment, usually executed by the Head Master or the Lower Master. The offender would have to pull down his trousers and pants and kneel on a block – the infamous Eton flogging block – with two 'holders' standing either side of him to restrain him in case he struggled. The ceremony was performed as a kind of ritual and was called, rather terrifyingly, an 'execution'. Most boys bit their lips and endured the pain but there was occasional struggling and screaming.

'The pain was spreading from the red-hot centre along all his nerves . . .'

Sport at Eton

Sport is an important part of school life at Eton and the boys take it very seriously. In fact, many Etonians have gone on to represent Great Britain internationally, including Sir Matthew Pinsent CBE, English rowing champion and four-time Olympic gold medallist. Most of the usual sports are played – rugby, soccer, cricket and rowing – and the school is known for its sporting champions. However, the school also has two of its own games, which are not played anywhere else.

The Wall Game

The Wall Game is a very old tradition (the earliest recorded game was played in 1766). It takes place at the school's southern wall, which was built in 1717. The game can seem incomprehensible to non-Etonians. As Pritpal comments:

'Nobody understands the rules.'

How to play: There are two teams of ten boys who play half-hour halves. The ball they use is like a football but with two slightly flattened sides. The teams play on a narrow strip of land, about 5 metres wide, which lies alongside the longer wall (110 metres long).

Play begins with a 'bully', like a rugby scrum. Players group together against the wall to try and take possession of the ball. The two sides then work their way – slowly and painfully, inch by inch – towards the ends of the wall, trying to move it away from their goal to their opponents' goal. The goals, known as *calx*, are special areas at each end of the wall.

Players are not allowed to handle the ball or to let any part of their bodies except their feet and hands touch the ground. They must not strike an opponent and there are also very strict 'offside' rules (such as no passing back and no playing in front). A player can score a 'shy' (one point) by raising the ball off the ground and against the wall with his foot. A team-mate must then touch the ball with his hand and shout 'Got it!'. Both these moves must happen within the calx area. The players can then attempt a 'goal' by throwing the ball at either a garden door or a tree, depending on which team they are on. This would earn them nine points.

(Fact) WALL GAME FACTS

■ *To see a goal scored is a rare sight – it only happens about once every ten years. Shies are slightly more common, about six a year.*

■ *The game may occasionally stop if the cry of 'Air' is heard. This means a player is suffocating under the crush of the scrum or bully.*

■ *Every St Andrew's Day (30 November) the school stages its Eton Wall Game match of the year. The last time a goal was scored at this match was in 1909.*

■ *In the nineteenth century, bare-knuckle boxing matches would take place close to the Wall, in a corner of College Field. Two boys would be matched against each other, usually for a grudge fight, and the punches would continue until one boy gave in. The poet Shelley once fought a school bully in one of these matches and gave him a good trouncing. Shelley was never bullied again. These fist-fights were stopped in 1825.*

The Field Game has been described as a bizarre combination of football and rugby. James is picked to play as a Forward for his House's lower boys' team because he is a fast runner and utterly fearless. After an exhausting and aggressive match, he finally manages to get the ball over the line.

'He was crushed from both sides and couldn't breathe.'

How to play: There are two teams of eleven players, with positions such as Forward, Post, Behind and Flying Man. The game starts with a bully, and one team 'has heads' – literally, having their heads down. The other team stand upright. The ball is rolled into the centre of the bully and, once it has exited, whoever gets possession tries to make their way to their opponents' goal. The ball is slightly smaller than a football, and players can never pick it up – not even the boys defending the goals. Players dribble the ball until it is taken from them. If an offence is committed, another bully takes place or a free kick is given.

If the ball is kicked between the posts and under the crossbar, this is a goal and worth three points.

A 'rouge' is a bit like a try in rugby. Worth five points, it is scored when the ball is kicked by an attacker, hits a defender, goes past the goal line and is touched down by an attacker. A rouge can also be scored if the ball is in a bully when it crosses the goal line.

A conversion (for two points) is taken after a rouge is scored. The attacking team can choose to have a 'ram', which is a line of three attackers behind each other. They run madly at the defending team, who protect the goal. Their aim is to get the ball over the goal line. The ram can be chaotic and, as James discovers, is basically a human battering-ram, hence the name.

'There was a loud thud as the leader's head battered into the enemy defenders.'

Eton Fives

Another sport played at the school is Eton Fives, a game that has roots in medieval times when peasants played with balls against chapel walls. No one is certain where the name comes from, but it probably refers to 'a bunch of fives', meaning hands.

Eton Fives has been played at the school since the seventeenth century and is a fast and furious game of hand-ball, played by four in two teams of 'doubles'. Players wear padded gloves to hit a rubber and cork ball against the walls. They play in a three-sided court, which has an unusually shaped interior containing buttresses, ledges and steps (based on the side of the chapel at Eton where the game was originally played). The variety of surfaces cause the ball to bounce off and change direction suddenly, creating an exciting and unpredictable game in which skill and experience count for more than strength and speed.

Less fun than Fives or the Field Game is the ordeal of the Eton school uniform. It really is torture for James. Not only is it uncomfortable, it is itchy, and fiddly to wear.

Boys shorter than 5 feet 4 inches (1.62 metres) had to wear the Eton suit, which had a short cropped jacket (known as a 'bum-freezer') and an Eton collar.

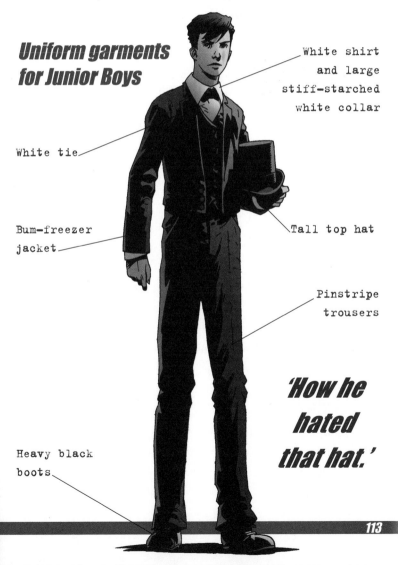

Uniform garments for Junior Boys

White shirt and large stiff-starched white collar

White tie

Bum-freezer jacket

Tall top hat

Pinstripe trousers

Heavy black boots

'How he hated that hat.'

The Bullies

Like all schools, Eton has its fair share of unpleasant types.

'But I told you, Bond, I'm going to kill you.'

Appearance: Sun-tanned and fit, with a strong jaw and gleaming teeth. But behind his healthy appearance, James senses that something isn't right about George Hellebore.

Background: Son of the loathsome Lord Hellebore, a rich industrialist who sets up a trophy called the Hellebore Cup for Eton. All three events are chosen so that George can win.

Character: George Hellebore is the first bully that James encounters at Eton. George takes an immediate dislike to James, especially when they become rivals in the Hellebore Cup. Later on board the train for Scotland, James is shocked when George attacks him and tries to throw him off the carriage. But as time goes on, James begins to feel sorry for the boy. His family circumstances – in particular, his bullying father and the performance-enhancing drugs he forces George to take – have turned him into a bully too. James decides there is hope for Hellebore.

Tony Fitzpaine

'Do you know who I am, you dirty little pleb?'

Appearance: Large boy with floppy hair, sticky-out ears and an arrogant sneer. Has an awful braying laugh, like a donkey.

Background: Known to be the son of someone important – possibly a duke or an earl – so has status at Eton. But is unpopular with the other boys.

Character: James comes across Fitzpaine when he catches him about to throw his friend Pritpal into the Thames. James punches Fitzpaine hard in the mouth and shoves him in the river instead, leaving him wallowing in the reeds. Unfortunately for James, a bitter and resentful Fitzpaine later resurfaces on the school trip to Sardinia, where he is chosen as James's opponent in a vicious boxing match. This is Fitzpaine's chance to get his revenge on James.

Theo Bentinck

'You have earned yourself a beating, Bond.'

Appearance: Pale and pimply, with dull brown hair and wire-framed spectacles. Has a grating nasal voice.

Background: One of the boys in charge of James's House – 'a bloodthirsty uncaring gang' – he is later promoted to Codrose's House Captain.

Character: 'Bloody Bentinck' has a reputation for being the worst bully of all. Pritpal knows him well – Bentinck

once beat him with a piece of rubber tubing, leaving him bleeding for two days afterwards. His crime? Being too noisy at breakfast. Bentinck takes great pleasure in punishing James, giving him five agonizingly painful lashes with a cane. Even James is shocked by the bleeding it causes.

THE ROYAL FAMILY

The Royal Family have always had a
connection with Eton. The school was
founded by a king, who paid for the
education of the original 70 pupils (there
are still 70 King's Scholars to this day),
and it fondly remembers its closest royal
patron, King George III, on his birthday.
The monarch on the throne at James's time,
King George V (who reigned from 1910 to
1936), also takes an interest in the
school and James discovers that he will
be making an unannounced visit to Eton on
the upcoming Fourth of June. While James
never meets the king, he is introduced to
his son, Prince Edward, at the Langton-
Herrings' party.

Prince Edward became king on 20 January
1936, following the death of his father.
But his reign was short-lived. After just
11 months he abdicated (gave up his right
to the throne) because he was in love with
an American woman called Wallis Simpson.
She had been married before and was a
divorcée, which put Edward, as King and
Supreme Governor of the Church of England,
in a difficult position. The public and the
Church would disapprove if he married her

and she would never be accepted as Queen. He chose instead to sacrifice the throne.

James also comes across a pair of little girls, the older of whom is called Lilibet. He climbs a tree and rescues a shuttlecock for her. James has no idea that the girls are the royal princesses, Elizabeth and Margaret. Elizabeth (Lilibet) would be crowned Queen Elizabeth II of England in 1953.

THE NAME OF WINDSOR

James's friend Miles Langton-Herring explains that the British Royal Family are originally from Germany. Queen Victoria was a Hanover, part of a German dynasty that came to England in 1714. During the First World War, King George V (Victoria's grandson) changed the family name of Saxe-Coburg-Gotha to Windsor, after the town. Having a German surname during the war — when the Germans were deadly enemies of Britain and her allies — did not seem appropriate. Since then, the Royal Family has been known by the name of Windsor.

James is certainly well travelled. Throughout his time at Eton he visits many different places, from the chilly Scottish Highlands to searingly hot Sardinia. But wherever James goes, adventure seeks him out.

During his first half at Eton, James receives a letter from Aunt Charmian, who is staying with his sick Uncle Max in the Scottish Highlands. She asks if James will come and spend his Easter holidays with them. James is more than happy to make the journey north. Travelling by train, he first arrives in London, where he picks up the overnight express to Fort William in the north-west of Scotland.

Capital city: Edinburgh Population: Approx. 5,144,200 Area: 30,414 km². Scotland has a land border with England, which runs for approximately 96km. Languages spoken: English, Gaelic, Scots Flag:

SCOTLAND ⌖ Short History

- *In ancient times, Scotland was populated by war-painted warriors called the Picts. Around AD 79 the Romans fought bloody battles against these fierce inhabitants, but they never conquered the whole country and they later built two huge walls – Hadrian's Wall and the Antonine Wall – to defend their territories.*

- *In the late thirteenth century the English King, Edward I, tried to take over Scotland, but at the Battle of Stirling Bridge an outnumbered Scottish army, led by William Wallace, defeated him in a savage battle that left at least 5,000 English dead. In 1314 Robert the Bruce again defeated a much larger English army at the Battle of Bannockburn, keeping a proud Scotland independent.*

- *In 1603 the crown of England passed to the Scottish King James VI who ruled both countries. Over 100 years later, in 1707, the Treaty of Union joined Scotland and England together as the United Kingdom. The Scottish Parliament was closed down and Scotland was governed from London. Riots broke out in Scotland. A rebellious Bonnie Prince Charlie and his army marched into England in 1745, but they were forced to retreat and were defeated at Culloden Moor in 1746, with the loss of many lives.*

- *In 1997 a vote showed that the people of Scotland wanted to have their own parliament. It was restored in May 1999.*

SCALE

0   30
ENGLISH MILES

Stornoʋ

THE
WESTERN
ISLES

ATLANTIC
OCEAN

NORTHEɪ
IRELANↃ

BY APPOINTMENT TO HIS MAJESTY

Orkney

Shetland

John o' Groats

NORTH
SEA

Moray Firth

Inverness

HIGHLANDS

Aberdeen

N

nw   ne

Fort William

SCOTLAND

W   E

sw   se

Antonine Wall

Firth of Forth

S

Glasgow

EDINBURGH (capital city)

of Clyde

LOWLANDS

Hadrian's Wall

Carlisle

Newcastle-upon-Tyne

ENGLAND

The London and North Eastern Railway

In the 1930s steam power was king and there was a large and much network of railway tracks across Britain. The London and North E. Railway was one of the 'Big Four' railway companies formed in 1923. It e for 25 years and covered a large area of Britain, running trains from L to the north-east of England and to Scotland.

• The LNER owned 7,700 locomotives. Its best-known locomotives were called Pacifics and they were associated with speed and luxury.

• The most famous Express Pacific was the Flying Scotsman, known for its distinctive bright green branding.

• The Flying Scotsman pulled passenger trains between London and Edinburgh from 1922. Because it could carry large supplies of coal, and pick up water while moving, it was the first train to travel the entire 633-kilometre journey without stopping. It was also the first steam engine to reach 100mph (160kmph) in 1934.

• Travelling on the train was a luxurious experience as it had a dining car, sleeping compartments and extra on-board services, such as a barber's shop.

EAST COAST ROUT

POPULA
ROUTE
BETWEEN
ENGLAN
AND
SCOTLAN
FROM & TO
LONDON
(KING'S CRO

How a steam train works

A steam train needs to have a very hot fire burning constantly. A fireman must shovel coal into the firebox throughout the journey to keep it going. On a long journey to Scotland, several tons of coal would have been needed and crew members would have shared the hard physical work of shovelling.

Tubes carry the heated air from the firebox to the boiler, which is full of water. The hot air heats the water until it becomes steam. The pressure from the steam pushes the pistons of the train backwards and forwards, which then move the connecting rods and turn the wheels. There is a chimney (a funnel) at the front of the train that carries the heated air and smoke out of the locomotive.

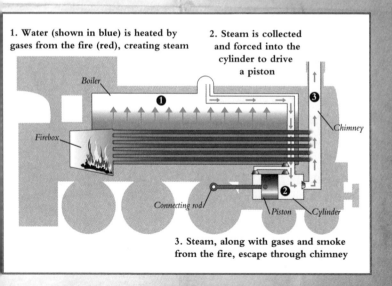

1. Water (shown in blue) is heated by gases from the fire (red), creating steam

2. Steam is collected and forced into the cylinder to drive a piston

Boiler

Firebox

Chimney

Connecting rod

Piston Cylinder

3. Steam, along with gases and smoke from the fire, escape through chimney

On a non-stop train like the Flying Scotsman, there would have been a scoop underneath that picked up water from a trough on the track as the train moved along.

The Steam Train to Scotland

James arrives at King's Cross to take the 7.39 London and North Eastern Railway Sleeping Car Express to Fort William in Scotland.

'Up ahead, the huge steam engine hissed and grumbled, waiting to be off.'

The train takes James, Red Kelly and George Hellebore more than 600 kilometres to the Scottish town of Fort William.

Meeting 'Red' Kelly

While boarding the train for Scotland, James notices a wiry red-haired boy hanging around. He asks James a favour – to keep the ticket collector busy while he slips on to the train.

'Kelly was a wild card, but James found it hard not to like him.'

The two lads meet up on the train and find they have something in common – they are both on their way to visit relatives in the village of Keithly in Scotland. Kelly is looking for his cousin Alfie, who has recently disappeared.

From then on, 'Red' Kelly – named for his distinctive shock of hair – and James become firm friends. Kelly is a few years older than James and comes from a large Irish family who have lived in London for a generation. With his cockney accent, sharp wit and cheeky, cheerful personality, James finds him very good company.

Despite his friendly exterior, Kelly has a tough side.

'James had no idea what Kelly had done to the big-eared boy, but he was down on the floor, curled up in a ball, gasping for breath and clutching his belly, his nose bleeding.'

James and Kelly pair up in Scotland, trying to piece together the mystery of Alfie's disappearance. Their investigations take them into some very dangerous territory. A firm trust is established between the boys and, when the Scottish trip finally comes to an end, James has a feeling that it isn't the last he's seen of Red Kelly.

The Scottish Highlands

James's first sight as the train draws into Fort William is Scotland's highest mountain, Ben Nevis, which is 1,344 metres above sea level. Aunt Charmian then drives him through the winding roads of the Highlands to Uncle Max's cottage in the small village of Keithly.

The mountainous regions of north and west Scotland are known as the Highlands. The scenery here is wild, dramatic and beautiful, with rocky mountains, deep valleys and long narrow lochs. There are also ruins of ancient castles and abbeys to explore. As James later discovers when he sinks into the boggy ground at Am Boglach Dubh (The Black Mire), peat bogs are common in this area. Peat can be dug up and burnt as fuel for crofts (small traditional farms) and distilleries (places where alcoholic drinks such as whisky are made). Less than twenty per cent of the Scottish population lives in the Highlands, mostly in scattered towns and villages.

Not far from Keithly lies the mysterious Castle Hellebore and Loch Silverfin, part of the rambling estate belonging to Lord Hellebore.

Castle Hellebore and Loch Silverfin

Situated on the edge of Loch Silverfin, Castle Hellebore stands on a small island connected to the mainland by a narrow causeway. It is a typical Scottish castle: tall, square and built of granite, with small turrets along some of the walls.

'In all it looked cold and mean and unwelcoming.'

Fact

SCOTTISH LOCHS

The most famous Scottish loch is an inland freshwater lake in north Scotland – the mysterious Loch Ness. It is the largest body of fresh water in Britain and also one of the deepest lochs in Scotland – 227 metres deep in places.

THE LOCH-NESS LEGEND

...nce the 1930s there have been reports, sightings ...d even blurry photographs taken of a huge, ...ssibly hump-backed, monster believed to live in ...e loch. But, despite much investigation, there ...as been no proper scientific evidence to back these ...tories up – yet. Some scientists believe the so-...alled 'monster' may actually be a very large fish ...alled a sturgeon.

Whatever the truth, Loch Ness is home to some very rare life forms, although they are tiny compared to its infamous monster. A total of 27 new species of nematode worm were recently discovered by Natural History Museum scientists in its muddy depths. The loch remains one of the largest unexplored environments in Europe.

Fishing in Scotland

Scotland is famed for its freshwater and sea fishing, having a multitude of freshwater lochs, rivers and streams, as well as a huge area of coastline with many inlets and sea lochs.

Uncle Max is a huge fan of a type of angling called fly-fishing, having bought the Keithly cottage (with full fishing rights) principally to pursue his favourite hobby. He is very keen to pass his enthusiasm on to James.

'When you stand in a river, fishing with a fly, you're part of nature, you're a heron, you're a kingfisher, you get to know the river like an old friend.'

Fly-fishing

Fly-fishing is a sport that makes use of an artificial fly as a lure. It is an ancient method best known for its success in catching trout and salmon, and it can be done in fresh or salt water, in lakes, streams or rivers.

Artificial flies are made by tying material such as feathers, hair or fur on to a hook with thread. These 'flies' can be matched in size, colour and pattern to the local insect life.

HOW TO FLY-FISH

A fly-fisherman uses a long, light rod called a fly rod, together with a reel, a line and a suitable fly. There are various lengths of rod and line, the choice dependent on the fish being caught and the local conditions. A leader is also used – a thin thread of material that attaches the fly to the end of the line. In this way the fly looks as if it is suspended in the water and the fish is fooled into thinking that it is real.

First, the fisherman needs to cast (or throw) the line out into the water. The most usual way is the forward (or overhead) cast, where the angler lifts the fly line into the air, flicks it back over the shoulder, then snaps it forward. As Max says, the action is 'like knocking a nail into a wall with a hammer'. The rod's movements are sometimes described as '10 to 2' - on the forward cast, the rod is at the 10 o'clock position while on the backward cast it is at 2 o'clock. The ideal cast should have the line tight at all times. It takes a lot of practice to get your fly to land smoothly and exactly where you want it in the water.

If a fish bites, the fisherman pulls in the line and lifts the rod tip. This 'sets' the hook inside the fish's mouth. The fisherman then needs to 'play' the fish by reeling up any slack line and then using the reel to pull the fish in. In this way, he can hopefully land the fish and have a good supper that night.

Landing a giant

The largest freshwater fish ever to be landed with a rod and line was a giant freshwater stingray, caught in the Maeklong River in Western Thailand in 2009. It took 90 minutes of hard struggling to bring the monster fish in. With a width of more than 2 metres and an estimated weight of more than 265kg, the stingray broke all records. It was eventually released back into the river.

Where to fish

Fish like to be sheltered and close to a food source. Here are some promising places to cast your line in a river or stream:

1. An area of fast-moving, shallow water is ideal – this part of the river or stream is called a riffle. There are a lot of insects here and the water is oxygenated, so fish will be attracted to this area. Even better fishing will be had where a riffle flows into deep water.

2. Fish like congregating beneath undercut river banks or shelves for protection, so this is another good place to choose. Look out for logs and rocks. Fish often swim behind or underneath them to wait for food to come by.

Whichever spot you decide on, bear in mind that fishing is a form of hunting, and the fisherman needs all the skills of the hunter. Stealth is the most important skill to learn. Sometimes a fish will bite straight away, other times you will need to be very patient and settle in for a long wait. Sometimes, of course, you will come away with nothing. James finds the wait frustrating but for Uncle Max, the long hours and the uncertain outcome are all part of the utter joy of fishing.

The Villains

'A little sadism before supper
will give me an appetite.'

Lord Randolph Hellebore

Origins: Born into a wealthy family, along with his brother Algar, Lord Hellebore inherited a castle and large estate in the Scottish Highlands that includes Loch Silverfin. He is the father of George Hellebore.

Hellebore is also the name of a plant, long used as a deadly poison. The word is a merging of 'hell' and 'bore' – most appropriate.

> *'As long as one man wants to bash another man's brains out, I'll be standing, ready to sell him a club.'*

Occupation: An arms dealer who once knew James's father, Hellebore is always on the hunt for an opportunity to make new and deadlier weapons. He aspires to create a stronger, more ruthless breed of warrior – a super-soldier – to unleash on the battlefield.

Appearance: Large and powerful, Hellebore is a striking figure who seems to exude health and vitality.

'Everything about the big man said that here was somebody rich and strong; here was somebody who felt he could rule the world. A true Roman emperor.'

Despite the gleaming white teeth, James recoils from Hellebore's stinking breath and animal-like odour. A hidden madness lurks behind Hellebore's eyes.

Interests: Loves sport of all kinds and inaugurates a new Eton trophy for the lower school, the Hellebore Cup. The event consists of three sports – running, swimming and shooting – all chosen so that his son George can excel.

Whereabouts: Highly protective of his land, Hellebore's castle is surrounded by armed staff and the utmost secrecy. His privacy is easily maintained, as the castle stands on a small island connected to the mainland by a narrow causeway. Hellebore makes occasional visits to Eton, mainly to bully his son.

Castle Hellebore is situated on the edge of Loch Silverfin, a vast, deep and uninviting lake. Named after a giant salmon from Scottish folklore – It'Airgid – the loch is shaped like a huge fish. Eels are known to swarm in its deep and murky waters.

'. . . hundreds of them, a seething mass in the water, balled up and tangled together like the writhing hair of some underwater Medusa.'

MONSTER EELS

Moray eels live in tropical seas and coral reefs. Growing up to a massive three metres long, they have strong, muscular bodies, ugly heads and very sharp teeth. It was recently discovered that moray eels have mobile jaws in their throats, which they can thrust forward to viciously bite their prey.

Moray eels can be aggressive but do not usually attack humans. However, one unfortunate diver, who was feeding sausages to a moray on a night-dive, had his thumb completely bitten off by the eel. The moray presumably thought it was just another sausage, but with more crunch.

The Romans were big fans of eating moray eels and would keep them in ponds in readiness for feasts. Roman author and naturalist Pliny the Elder wrote about the Roman emperor Vitellius, who had a taste for the exotic and once ate a dish of parrot livers, peacock brains, flamingo tongues and the spleens of moray eels.

Cleek MacSawney

Origins: The name Cleek MacSawney has connections even more unpleasant than the man himself – two infamous Scottish cannibals, Christie Cleek and Sawney Bean. In the fourteenth century Christie was thought to be part of a group who attacked travellers on the passes of the Grampian Mountains. Tearing into his victims with a hook on a rod (known as a 'cleke') he would then consume their bodies. Sawney also liked to feast on innocent travellers. He and his cannibalistic family were supposed to have lived in a cave and captured hundreds of people for their meals.

Occupation: Lord Hellebore's gillie (a Scottish Gaelic term for a right-hand man who assists on hunting and fishing expeditions). Born and bred locally, MacSawney enjoys hunting and trapping. He doesn't much care if the prey is animal or human.

Appearance: MacSawney's short height and over-long arms give him the appearance of an ape – one wearing a gamekeeper's jacket and a battered bowler hat.

'His skin had the appearance of boiled ham, the fat squashy end of his long nose had great gaping pores and the whites of his watery eyes were permanently pink.'

The Villains

Dr Perseus Friend

Origins: Born in Germany to an Irish father and a Russian mother. Perseus's father was a scientist of dubious reputation. During the First World War he developed poison gas for use in the trenches. After the war, he travelled the world with Perseus, creating chemical weapons for anyone willing to pay him. The father–and–son team ended up in Russia developing germ warfare in Soviet laboratories.

POISON GAS IN THE GREAT WAR

Poison gas was first used on a large scale by the Germans during the First World War. On 22 April 1915, Allied soldiers on the Western Front at Ypres, France, spotted clouds of mysterious yellowy-green gas drifting towards them. The effects were devastating. Soldiers began choking as they inhaled the chlorine gas. Once ingested, the gas reacted with water to form hydrochloric acid, which ate away their lungs. Troops fled in panic and a large gap was left open in the Allied line. Many died in that first attack and gas masks were quickly rushed to soldiers at the front.

In retaliation, the British prepared their own gas attack, which took place at Loos in September. But it went badly wrong when the wind blew the gas back into the British trenches. By the end of the attack, there were reckoned to be more Allied casualties than German.

After the war, when the world had fully seen the horrific damage that poison gas could wreak upon humans, a treaty called the Geneva Protocol (1925) came into force. This banned the future use of chemical and biological weapons.

Occupation: Following in his father's footsteps, Perseus became interested in germ warfare and now works obsessively in this field. But his interests are not confined to bacteria. His work with Hellebore involves developing hormone-based serums that cause horrific mutations in humans and animals.

> ## 'He never experienced love, or hate, or sadness, or happiness, or even anger – unless an experiment went wrong or his work was interrupted by some inconvenience.'

Appearance: A thin pale man, slightly balding but still with a few strands of wispy blond hair. He has a habit of continually polishing his wire-framed glasses. Perseus also has an exceptionally dull, droning voice.

Hormones and growth

Hormones are chemical messengers that are naturally produced by the body and carried in the bloodstream. They regulate the workings of the organs and cells.

One powerful hormone regulates growth. If the wrong amount of this hormone is produced in children, it has a drastic effect on their development. Too little and the child may not grow enough. Too much and gigantism may occur, whereby the child grows very large.

The most famous giant was Robert Wadlow, born in 1918, who was the size of an adult by the age of 5. When he was 22 he was a towering 2.72m tall and weighed 220kg.

Patients can be treated with growth hormone by doctors. The hormone is made by genetic engineering – when the genes found in all living things are altered by scientists. Before genetic engineering, the only way to get this hormone was to extract it from a human corpse.

Robert Wadlow compared to his father, Harold Wadlow

Genetic engineering has also been used to develop growth hormone for other purposes. In cows and pigs, for example, hormones have been developed to make them produce more milk and leaner meat. Scientists are also trying to find ways of using these hormones to prevent or slow down the effects of ageing in humans. Growth hormone can also increase muscle size and improve performance for athletes who rely on strength. However, the use of human growth hormone in sport is banned by the International Olympic Committee.

Origins: His Excellency Count Ugo Carnifex was born into humble beginnings in Sardinia but always had big ambitions.

Occupation: Ugo fought for the Italians during the First World War, where he met Zoltan the Magyar, fighting for the Austro-Hungarians. About to shoot each other, they were distracted by the sight of treasure. When they decided to steal it together, Ugo's brother objected. The Count stabbed him savagely in the back.

'A little sadism before supper will give me an appetite.'

Appearance: A tall pale figure dressed in pristine white. With his milky white skin and silver tooth, Ugo presents an unsettling, ghostly picture.

Whereabouts: The self-styled count can be found in his magnificent palazzo in the Barbagian mountains of central Sardinia. He loves art and likes to surround himself with beautiful things, usually stolen to order.

Other characteristics: Ugo speaks Latin and is the leader of a mysterious society called the Milennaria. The Milennaria seek to rebuild the Roman Empire, and return to the glorious times when Rome ruled the world. They originally launched their underground campaign in 1900, exactly two thousand years after the birth of Julius Caesar.

SECRET SOCIETIES

Secret societies have existed for hundreds of years all over the world. Despite their different objectives all secret societies have one thing in common. Their members must conceal their activities – and sometimes their identities – from the outside world.

THE BEATI PAOLI

Beati Paoli means 'the Blessed People'. They were a secret organization of intellectuals and noblemen believed to have existed in the 1600s in Sicily. Their aim was to stand up against the corrupt authorities in power, and they took vows to avenge any wrongdoing.

Wearing black hooded cloaks, they worked under cover of night, kidnapping suspects and taking them back to their underground meeting places in the catacombs of Palermo. There they would conduct a 'trial' and decide on an appropriate punishment. For many years the name Beati Paoli struck fear into people's hearts and some believe they were the forefathers of the infamous Sicilian Mafia.

THE KRYPTEIA
The name comes from the Greek, meaning 'secret things'.
In Ancient Greece the city of Sparta had an extremely
powerful army and the *Krypteia* was their secretive and
ancient rite of passage, a kind of test to prove if a
man was worthy of greater things. Promising and educated
young Spartan men, aged about 18, were sent out into the
countryside at night, completely naked and armed with a
knife. They were told to survive by any means necessary.
Those who survived this punishing test of manhood were
welcomed into the tough Spartan Army.

THE FREEMASONS
The Freemasons form a huge global organization with
approximately 6 million members. Founded in England
600 years ago, it is a highly secretive society — very
difficult to penetrate if you are not a member. Those
wanting to join must be elected by existing Masons in
a secret ballot.

Masons are forbidden from letting anyone outside the
society know about its activities, or the identities
of other members. Known to follow a strict moral code
of fellowship and behaviour, they also have to swear
allegiance to a 'supreme being'. They carry out a
complex series of rituals and ceremonies. A Mason can
identify a fellow Mason through their infamous secret
handshake.

THE FIVE POINTS OF FELLOWSHIP
'Foot to foot': to go to help your brother Mason
'Knee to knee': pray for your brother Mason
'Breast to breast': keep the secrets
'Hand to back': assist your fallen brother Mason
'Mouth to ear': whisper good counsel

Ugo Carnifex was not the only person to have dreams of recreating the glorious Roman Empire. The Italian leader Benito Mussolini (1883–1945) was a huge admirer of Ancient Rome and he incorporated many of its ideas during his rule.

Mussolini was a dictator who stood alongside Hitler during the Second World War. A dictator is an oppressive ruler who has absolute power. But in Roman times the name did not have this meaning – a dictator was simply a magistrate who was given temporary powers. It was Julius Caesar who abused these powers when he made himself a magistrate and kept the title permanently. From then on, the word 'dictator' began to have a negative meaning.

Mussolini seized power in Italy in 1922 during his famous March on Rome. He and his Fascist party proceeded to rule the country with an iron fist. Authority was enforced by the Blackshirts – ex-soldiers who made sure no one opposed the great man. Their motto '*Me ne frego*' means 'I don't give a damn'.

Just like the glory days of the Roman Empire, Mussolini wanted to build a nation of warriors. And he believed in starting young. Children were expected to join youth groups that told them how they should behave and what to aim for in life. Boys were to be fierce soldiers who would fight for Italy, while girls should want to become mothers who would provide the next generation of Italians. Like the Romans, a child in one of these groups was called a *legionary* (an adult was a *centurion*).

Mussolini often used quotes from the ancient Roman poets in his rousing speeches. And he adopted the Roman salute for the Fascist party: an extended straight arm with a flat hand, palm facing down, raised high in front of the body. This was a tribute to the ancient empire that was famed for its conquests and far-reaching power.

When the Second World War came to an end in 1945 Mussolini was executed by shooting.

Ugo's funicular railway

In order to reach the high palazzo, Ugo has had two funicular railways built – steep railway lines capable of easily transporting people or goods up or down a hill or mountain.

HOW IT WORKS

The word 'funicular' comes from the roman for funiculus, *which means 'thin rope'. This refers to the cables system that moves the cars up and down.*

Funicular railways operate on a simple counterweight system – the ascending and descending cars move in opposite directions at the same time, thereby counterbalancing each other.

Originally, funiculars of this type had to have running water available at the top of the incline to power a turbine. But most modern funiculars are operated by electric engines.

Both cars are the same weight. When the descending car is heavier with passengers, its weight can be used to pull the lighter car up the incline. If the ascending car is heavier, the engine only needs to pull the weight of the extra passengers, as the weight of the two cars will always cancel each other out.

The drive wheel is powered by an engine.

⬤ *The world's steepest passenger railway is the Katoomba Scenic Railway in New South Wales, Australia. Built in 1878, it has a nerve-racking incline of 52 degrees. Passengers ascend backwards up a 415-metre cliff, enjoying spectacular rainforest views.*

⬤ *The oldest water-powered (and still operational) funicular in the world is Bom Jesus in Braga, Portugal, built in 1882. At 274 metres long, it has a gradient of 42 degrees.*

⬤ *There is a famous Italian song called 'Funiculi, Funiculà'. On first hearing, one might think it is a romantic song about love. But in fact, it is just about a funicular railway.*

Zoltan the Magyar

Origins: Raised in Hungary. Fought in the First World War against the Italians. Ran away to Greece and, after falling in with criminals, became master of his own ship by pushing its captain overboard. Coming from a country without a coastline, Zoltan fears the sea. Many sailors thought it was bad luck to learn to swim. And Zoltan agrees.

'I will never swim. I fight the sea. I have mastered the sea. I sail my boat upon it, and I will not put myself into its mouth.'

Occupation: A pirate and captain of his boat *Charon*, Zoltan smuggles drugs, guns and other contraband across the Mediterranean. He also steals works of art for Ugo Carnifex.

Appearance: Distinctive with short blond hair and startling silvery-grey eyes. Zoltan has a strong muscular build.

Other characteristics: Zoltan is fiercely patriotic and loves his country. Ruthless but simple, he dreams of making enough money to stop smuggling and retire. He develops a strong bond with Amy Goodenough while holding her captive.

'I killed her father. That is not a good way to win a girl's heart.'

THE GOLDEN AGE OF PIRACY

Pirates began operating in the Caribbean in the late seventeenth century. They were attracted by Spanish merchant ships known as galleons, which were carrying huge amounts of treasure back to Spain following the Spanish conquest of the Americas – incredible cargoes of silver, gold, jewels and precious spices. The pirates would attack by getting close to their target ship, throwing grappling hooks on to it, and catching it like a gigantic fish.

There were other kinds of pirates called privateers. They sailed on privately owned ships and were paid by countries to attack and rob enemy ships. Privateers would often split whatever they pillaged with the countries that commissioned them. One of the most famous privateers was Henry Morgan, who was commissioned by the British government to carry out attacks against the Spanish. He had a fearsome reputation and was said to hang men by their genitals as a punishment.

If a pirate was captured by the authorities he was usually sentenced to hanging – a slow and agonizing death that often took several minutes. This would be done in public to show people the evils of piracy.

Piracy is becoming a big problem in some parts of the world. Today's pirates are usually violent and well-organized gang members who have machine guns, speedboats and hi-tech computers at their disposal. There have been 3,583 pirate attacks on boats and ships since 1992 and many crew members have been injured and killed by the pirates. One of the world's most notorious areas for pirate attacks is off the coast of Somalia – in April 2009 Somali pirates kidnapped an American ship's captain and demanded a £1.6 million ransom for his safe return. Fortunately, he was rescued by the US Navy but three of the pirates were killed during the operation.

Sir John Charnage

*'What do you think your epitaph should be?
How about "Here lies a boy who couldn't keep
his nose out of other people's business"?'*

Origins: Born into a wealthy family, John Charnage read chemistry at Cambridge. Now he lives in a grand house in Berkeley Square, London, where he keeps a macabre collection of poisons in glass jars – among them black widow spider venom and deadly nightshade.

Occupation: Overseeing the creation of NEMESIS, the vast code-breaking machine he has been building for the Russians. But Charnage doesn't have the knowledge to finish it alone.

Appearance: Despite dressing in an expensive cravat and smoking-jacket, Sir John has an unhealthy appearance about him, with his pale greyish skin, sleepy eyes and nicotine-stained fingers.

Interests: Sir John spends his leisure time drinking, smoking and gambling.

POISONOUS DEATHS

Lined up in their gloomy cabinet, the labels on Sir John's poison jars read like a list of famous historical deaths. Poison has long been used by the powerful and mighty to rid themselves of enemies and rivals. It was easy to use, convenient and the crime would often go undetected.

☠ *The favoured poison of the powerful and ruthless Borgia family in Renaissance Italy was arsenic – 'the king of poisons, the poison of kings'. The Borgias were said to have poisoned numerous dinner party guests with their tainted wine. The guests would not have suspected a thing as arsenic is extremely difficult to detect, being colourless, odourless and tasteless. But it is an incredibly potent chemical. Once swallowed, terrible nausea, vomiting and diarrhoea begin, which lead to eventual death.*

☠ *Hemlock was the poison that killed Socrates, the famous philosopher of Athens, who was sentenced to death in 399 BC for corrupting the city's youth and interfering with its religion. Socrates was effectively his own executioner, apparently drinking the cup of hemlock he was given by the authorities. Plato, his friend, described how a deadly chill seemed to spread through Socrates' body as he slowly died. Hemlock poison comes from the plant of the same name and is highly toxic, causing muscular paralysis and eventually depriving the heart of oxygen.*

☠ *Cyanide, a chemical that can exist in different forms, has always had a reputation for being utterly deadly. It is particularly known as a fast-acting suicide device used by secret agents in the event of them being captured by the enemy. It was also used by spies to perform assassinations. In the 1960s the KGB (an organization once in charge of Russian security) even devised a walking stick that could fire a deadly shot of cyanide at a chosen victim. Cyanide works quickly by making the body unable to use oxygen. In the closing days of the Second World War, Adolf Hitler, holed up in a bunker and confronted with defeat, used both cyanide and a gun to kill himself.*

NEMESIS
The Plans

- -

The NEMESIS machine is the invention that Sir John has been working on for years.

NAME:

Numeric
Evaluating
Mathematical
Engine and
Serial
Intelligence
System.

WHAT IT IS:

NEMESIS is a million times more intelligent than any human. Any country or organization that gets hold of it would have an incredibly powerful weapon in their hands. Why? Because NEMESIS can produce the ultimate in intelligence – a code that can never be broken.

- -

'No man has ever been able to invent a code
that couldn't be broken, but a machine
might just do it.'

THE SECRET OF BLETCHLEY PARK

Throughout the Second World War, both the Allies and the Axis powers encrypted their messages so that the enemy would not be able to understand them. Top-secret information would be written in code or cipher, both forms of secret communication called cryptology.

Teams of experts were employed by both sides to try and decrypt enemy information. In Britain, 12,000 code-breakers worked at Bletchley Park, a country house in Buckinghamshire requisitioned by the intelligence services. Known as Station X, it was surrounded by secrecy. Among the team was Alan Turing, one of a group of brilliant mathematicians and puzzle-solvers whose job it was to crack the German ciphers. Turing's ground-breaking work earned him the name 'father of computer science'.

The ENIGMA machine

The Germans encrypted their information using a cipher machine called ENIGMA, which they believed was impossible to crack. ENIGMA used rotors whose movement produced constantly changing substitutions for the alphabet. However, after years of work, Bletchley Park code-breakers succeeded in cracking ENIGMA. This was an amazing feat, and Turing's work had been the key. Building on the work of Polish mathematicians, he had developed an electro-mechanical machine, which was essentially an early version of a computer. It was called the Bombe – because of the scarily loud ticking noise it made while it was working. Today all digital computers work on the same principle as Turing's machine.

This success meant that by 1942 Bletchley Park teams were decoding about 39,000 intercepted enemy messages every month. The information they gained was key in bringing an end to the war and saving thousands of lives.

How to Crack a Cipher

Breaking a difficult code or cipher can be a complicated business. A code-breaker needs to be very intelligent and extremely patient, as the work can take a very long time. But the basic principles of codes and ciphers are actually quite simple.

Codes and ciphers – what's the difference?

1. A code replaces complete words or phrases with other words, numbers or symbols. The names of secret agents and missions are usually in code, to hide their identity. In his adventures, James comes across spies called Diamond and Obsidian and a top-secret plot coded as Operation Snowblind.
2. A cipher is based on single letters, substituted by other letters, numbers or symbols or completely rearranged.

To break a code you need to have a code book or key to help you, while ciphers can be unscrambled using a variety of different methods.

A good way of starting to break a cipher is to see how often certain letters appear in a message. The most common letters in English are E, T, A, O and N. If you check a simple cipher for letter frequency, the letter that comes up most often will usually represent E. The second most common letter would be T, and so on. The code-breaker may be able to identify obvious words using just the common letters, then filling in the gaps (a bit like a crossword puzzle). There are also common words like THE and AND that are easier to identify. Once the cipher has been broken, other messages sent using the same system can easily be read.

Julius Caesar used a simple cipher, also known as a *shift cipher*, for sending messages to his generals. He moved the alphabet along a certain number of places so that a different letter was substituted for the letter he wanted to use. This is an easy cipher to create – simply decide how many places you want to move along, using a second alphabet as a guide. The cipher below starts three places along so that the letter A is represented by D. The word HELLO would read KHOOR in a message.

A	B	C	D	E	F	G	H	I	J	K	L	M	N	O	P	Q	R	S	T	U	V	W	X	Y	Z
D	E	F	G	H	I	J	K	L	M	N	O	P	Q	R	S	T	U	V	W	X	Y	Z	A	B	C

One way of making the cipher much more difficult to decrypt is to change the lengths of each word. Common two-letter words can easily be identified, such as TO or AN. But if you put all your letters together and then divide them up into chunks – five letters is the usual number – it makes it much harder for the code-breaker.

```
For example,
MEET ME AT HIGHGATE CEMETERY
would become
PHHW PH DW KLJKJDWH FHPHWHUB
and divided into five-letter chunks is
PHHWP HDWKL JKJDW HFHPH WHUB
```

Wolfgang and Ludwig Smith

'I pride myself on a clean death when it's necessary.'

Origins: Named after the famed composers Wolfgang Amadeus Mozart and Ludwig van Beethoven, the two brothers decided not to follow their parents into a musical career. Instead they joined the infamous and ruthless London gang known as the Sabinis.

Occupation: The brothers are violent thugs available for hire, currently working for Sir John Charnage.

Appearance: Older brother Ludwig is so gaunt and thin, he looks like a skeleton. His horribly over-sized bony head adds to his grotesque appearance, with his black eyes peering out from dark hollow sockets. Wolfgang, however, looks relatively normal with an ordinary face and build.

Gangs of the East End

London, like all big cities, has always been a magnet for crime. The East End was once particularly notorious for its criminal element, and was crawling with burglars, pickpockets, forgers and, of course, street gangs.

In the early twentieth century, Whitechapel in London's East End was dominated by two violent Russian immigrant gangs: the Odessians and the Bessarabian Tigers. In the nineteenth century many Russians had come to live in London and, while most of them tried to make an honest living, some decided there was an easier way to make money. The gangs preyed on hardworking locals by running protection rackets – people such as shop owners had to pay a regular fee as 'protection' to the gang. If anyone objected, they would be attacked with guns, knives or broken bottles.

As the gangs battled for control, violence broke out in the streets. A big-time Bessarabian called Perkoff was lured into an alley and had one of his ears savagely sliced off by an Odessian. Revenge attacks soon took place and in 1902 the violence culminated in a massive fight at a music hall, where one of the Odessians was stabbed to death. After this, the leaders were imprisoned and eventually the gangs broke up.

Also operating at the turn of the century was the Blind Beggar Gang, which was based in a pub of the same name. (In later years, the Blind Beggar pub would become notorious as the place where a gangster called Ronnie Kray cold-bloodedly shot George Cornell, a member of a rival gang.) The Blind Beggar Gang were a team of highly skilled pickpockets, around twenty in total, who for years stole from unwary victims in the Petticoat Lane area of the city.

Fact

THE SAVAGE SABINIS

One of the most famous East End gangs in the 1920s and 30s was, of course, the Sabinis, who with their Italian-Irish heritage were probably the closest thing London had to a Mafia. Headed by Charles 'Darby' Sabini, they were based in Little Italy in Clerkenwell. However, their main business was done at the horse racecourses of Epsom, Brighton and Lewes. Protection rackets, organized robberies, loan-sharking (lending money to the desperate, and demanding huge amounts of interest on return) – the Sabinis did it all.

When it came to fighting, the Sabinis' preferred weapon was the barbershop razor, appropriately known as the 'cut-throat'. The racing business was highly lucrative so if anyone tried to move in on the Sabinis' turf they would retaliate with savage stabbings, slashings and shootings. Full-scale battles between dozens of razor-wielding thugs would occasionally take place at the racecourse meetings and the Sabinis continued to operate for almost twenty years.

El Huracán

Origins: Born in a village deep in the rainforest of southern Mexico and named after Hurakan, the Mayan god of wind and storms. His Spanish name 'El Huracán' – 'The Hurricane' – was earned in his military days due to his fearsome reputation for destroying everything in his path.

Occupation: Mysterious self-styled head of Lagrimas Negras, an isolated island in the Caribbean transformed into a luxurious hide-out for international criminals on the run. But El Huracán only gives shelter to those who can pay him handsomely.

Appearance: Well-dressed in the style of a Mexican aristocrat, El Huracán's Mexican-Indian heritage is reflected in his dark brown skin and a face with the appearance of having been carved out of old dark wood. With his pure white hair and Vandyke beard, El Huracán exudes a cool elegance.

Interests: El Huracán enjoys the finer things in life: luxurious surroundings, good cigars, the best-quality food and drink. A clever and cultured man, he is extremely knowledgeable about the history of the ancient Mayans.

Other characteristics: Merciless to those he believes have betrayed him. Rather than shoot his enemies, he prefers to see them die a long drawn-out death in *La Avenida de la Muerte* – the Avenue of Death. This torturous rat-run is El Huracán's own creation.

Whereabouts: Last seen at the Lagrimas Negras harbour. The mysterious island of Lagrimas Negras was once a penal colony, a place where runaways, slaves and troublemakers were imprisoned – hence its name, meaning 'black tears'.

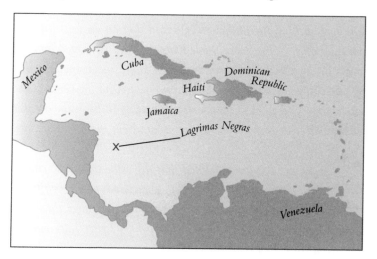

El Huracán bought the island – his father's birthplace – from the Americans for $35,000. Then he put the word around that this was the place to come if you were on the run and needed a place to hide out – but at a price.

Fact

THE REAL-LIFE ISLAND ESCAPE

Alcatraz is a small rocky island in the middle of San Francisco Bay in California. Because of its isolated position, it was once used as a high-security prison by the US authorities. Many of America's most notorious criminals and gang leaders were jailed here (including the famous gangster Al Capone) as it was believed to be the most secure and escape-proof environment possible.

This didn't prevent four prisoners from hatching an ingenious escape plan in 1962. Criminals Frank Lee Morris, brothers John and Clarence Anglin and Allen West took months to execute their idea. They knew that there was a small corridor that was less than a metre wide behind their adjacent cells and that an air vent led there from their cells. Using home-made tools – a drill fashioned from the motor of a broken prison vacuum cleaner and a metal spoon – they dug and chipped away at the damp concrete around the vents. It was quite a noisy operation so they took turns doing shifts in the evening. A false wall was used to conceal their work from the prison guards.

On June 11, Morris decided that the grille was loose enough to make an escape that night. But West had fallen behind in his digging and didn't make it out in time. The other three men disappeared into the night, taking with them water rafts and life jackets that they had made from fifty raincoats, along with a home-made pump with which to inflate the raft. As a decoy, they left behind life-size dummies in their beds, made from a papier-mâché mixture of cement, soap and toilet paper. The dummies had painted skin, faces and real hair that had been taken from the prison barbers. Two of the dummies even had names – Oink and Oscar.

Morris and the Anglin brothers were never seen again. The FBI concluded that the men had drowned in the cold waters of the bay. They were the only people to escape the prison in its years of operation.

Mrs Theda Glass

'I guess you could call me a spy.'

Occupation: Female mercenary smuggling secrets all over the world for anyone that pays her. Currently leads a gang searching for stolen US naval documents to sell to the Japanese.

Appearance: Blonde, beautiful. Mrs Glass is always seen wearing a hat and a scarf on her head. Rumour has it she is partly bald due to a past machine-gun attack strafing her head.

'You cause us any trouble and I will personally shoot your eyes out and use your heads as bowling balls. *Comprende?*'

LADIES WITH GUNS

Not all gangsters in history have been male. Like Mrs Glass, some women have shown themselves to be just as expert as the guys when it comes to crime, guns and shooting.

MA BARKER

Kate 'Ma' Barker was the notorious head of a gang who committed many violent crimes throughout the 1920s and 30s in America. The gang were actually members of her own family, comprising her four sons: Herman, Lloyd, Arthur and Freddie. (Mr Barker, Ma's husband, had been abandoned for being a worthless drunk.)

The gang began by robbing banks and hijacking postal deliveries, then moved on to kidnapping which they found even mor lucrative. They shot anyone wh stood in their way, even innocer bystanders, and they soo earned themselves a frightenin reputation.

In 1935 there was a fierce gu battle between FBI agents and M Barker who was with one of he sons. The Barkers fought it ou but were eventually shot dead b the agents. According to the FB report, a tommy gun was found i the hands of the dead Ma Barker.

onícle

Post

BONNIE AND CLYDE

Bonnie Parker and her boyfriend Clyde Champion Barrow were a young couple who were believed to have committed thirteen murders and numerous robberies and burglaries during a two-year crime spree. The pair travelled through five states of America, robbing banks, petrol stations, shops and fruit stands as they went. They often stole cars to make their getaway.

Despite the fact that they terrorized shop-owners and shot at those who got in their way, Bonnie and Clyde caught the imagination of Americans at the time. The USA was suffering from the Great Depression and people enjoyed reading about the wayward lawless couple, who took whatever they wanted, whenever they wanted.

But in 1934 Bonnie and Clyde were ambushed by police officers in Louisiana following a major manhunt. They were shot repeatedly, some reports say up to fifty times each. And when their Ford was inspected afterwards, a cache of weapons was discovered, including automatic rifles, semi-automatic shotguns and various types of handgun. It also contained fifteen car licence plates from different states.

Bonnie and Clyde loved taking photos of themselves, especially posing gangster-style with shotguns, so there are many photos of the criminal couple. Their story remains a legend in the USA.

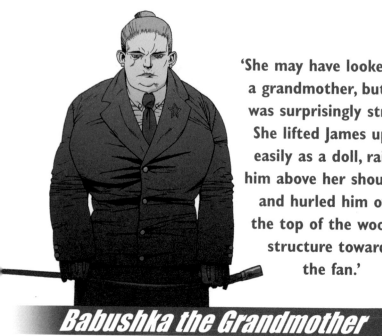

'She may have looked like a grandmother, but she was surprisingly strong. She lifted James up as easily as a doll, raised him above her shoulders and hurled him over the top of the wooden structure towards the fan.'

Babushka the Grandmother

Origins: Born on a farm in the Ukraine, she fought fiercely in the First World War and the Russian Revolution. Later joined the Obedinennoe Gosudarstvennoe Politicheskoe Upravlenie (OGPU) – otherwise known as the Russian Secret Police. Her real name is Colonel Irena Sedova. Babushka means 'grandmother' in Russian.

Occupation: A Russian spymaster who runs a network of spies and secret agents throughout Europe, undermining foreign governments and ruthlessly eliminating those who might want to harm the communist regime.

Appearance: Very sturdy and solidly built, at first appearance Babushka looks like an ordinary grey-haired peasant woman. Dresses in grey from top to toe, with thick stockings and lace-up boots. Underneath she is solid muscle and fat. Wears a steel-enforced corset underneath her clothes to protect her from enemy bullets.

THE RUSSIAN SECRET POLICE

For many years Russia used its vast network of secret police to be informers on the Russian people. The secret police had huge power over people's lives and so were greatly feared. The organization underwent many name changes over the years, but their task remained more or less the same: to suppress any rebellious activity and thought.

It was first organized in 1825 at the order of Czar Nicholas I and members of the secret police would sometimes impersonate revolutionaries when going undercover. After the Russian Revolution in 1917, the government began a new secret police force called Cheka, which became incredibly feared. It was later reorganized as the GPU, then the OGPU, of which Babushka is a leading member.

The OGPU's aim was to stop any further revolutions from happening in Russia, unearth political rebels and, later, to enforce collective farming among the people. (Babushka's cover as part of a trade delegation selling Soviet tractors is certainly convincing.) The OGPU had its own army and a vast network of spies. It became part of the NKVD in 1934.

The Secret Police and the Great Terror
During the 1930s, the Russian leader Joseph Stalin ordered massive purges on the Russian people. Any person considered to be disloyal

to the state could be sent to a prison
camp, murdered or put on trial and made
to confess to all kinds of crimes — this
period is known as the Great Terror.
Stalin's secret police, the NKVD, were
responsible for making arrests and around
20 million Russians were sent to the
notorious Gulag — labour camps in Siberia
— where many died in terribly harsh and
freezing conditions. Christians, members of
ethnic groups, artists, intellectuals and
many more were all persecuted. And ordinary
people could be arrested by the NKVD for
the most trivial crimes, such as telling a
joke about Stalin or being late for work.
It was no wonder that people lived in
constant fear and suspicion of those around
them. In later years, the Russian secret
police were known as the KGB.

Vladimir Wrangel

Wrangel is a clever, ambitious Russian
who goes by the alias of Agent Amethyst.
He is believed to work for a top-secret
communist cell headed by Babushka.
However, Wrangel is surrounded by mystery
— he moves swiftly and silently to get
any job, even murder, done effectively.

England's Russian Spies

In the 1930s a group of young men studying at Cambridge University were recruited as Russian spies. Their names were Philby, Blunt, Burgess, Maclean and Carincross, and they are now known as the Cambridge Spies. The eldest, Anthony Blunt, was recruited by the NKVD during a trip to Russia in 1933, and he went on to recruit others to the cause. All five men lived most of their lives undiscovered, and it was only many years later that their treachery was exposed.

The men came from privileged backgrounds and were intelligent and highly educated. Over time, they had come to believe that capitalism was corrupt and that the ideals of the Soviet Union offered a better alternative. In choosing to work for the Soviets, they betrayed and deceived their families and friends — and, of course, their country — because they believed they were serving a greater cause.

Double – or Treble – Agents?

During their long careers, the Cambridge Spies were classic double agents — pretending to be working for British interests, but in fact serving the Russians. They did a great deal of damage, though no one will ever know exactly how much. During the Second World War, for example, Burgess and Blunt transmitted Foreign Office and MI5 documents

that outlined top-secret details of
Allied military strategy. Kim Philby, who
worked in Intelligence for MI6, informed
the Russians that the Nazi secret code
ENIGMA had been broken by his colleagues
at Bletchley Park. He also told the KGB
about British agents who were operating in
Russia. Ironically, Philby was actually the
director of anti-Soviet counterintelligence
for the British from 1944 to 1946.

All these men had important jobs in key
organizations, including the Foreign Office
and MI5. This meant that the Russians had
access to the highest-level information.
It seems unbelievable that the spies
managed to deceive everyone around them for
so many years. The Cambridge Spies clearly
excelled in their roles, but even though
they were loyal to Moscow, the KGB did not
fully trust them. Could they in fact have
been treble agents – seemingly loyal to
Moscow but actually serving the British
intelligence services that they were
supposed to be betraying? The Cambridge
Spies probably never realized the full
extent of the KGB's distrust.

Location: Sardinia

James's summer trip to Sardinia is supposed to be a relaxing experience, a way to 'get away from dreary old England' as Aunt Charmian puts it. James plans to spend a few days on Mr Haight's school expedition, then visit his cousin Victor on the coast at Capo d'Orso.

He travels by steamer from Italy to Terranova, and meets the Eton boys at Torralba to begin exploring the ancient monuments of Sardinia. But, as usual, James's holiday turns out to be anything but relaxing . . .

Capital city: Cagliari Population: Approx. 1,655,600
Area: 30,414 km². Most of Sardinia is a mountainous plateau that slopes to the sea.
Languages spoken: Sardinian, Italian Flag:

SARDINIA — Short History

- *The island of Sardinia has survived hordes of invaders throughout its turbulent history. Drawn to the island's strategic trading position in the Mediterranean Sea, as well as its natural riches (among them, valuable silver, iron and lead deposits), plundering pirates and foreign invaders have attacked its shores time and again.*

- *Originally inhabited by the mysterious Nuraghic civilization from 1800 BC, Phoenicians, Carthaginians, Romans, Arabs, Byzantines and Saracens all followed but the powerful Romans ruled the longest. In 1861 Sardinia became part of the unified Italian state and later gained its own government.*

- *The invaders have all left their distinctive mark on the culture, language and architecture of the island, and ancient monuments, settlements, temples and tombs dot the Sardinian countryside.*

SCALE

0   15
ENGLISH MILES

Alghe

THE ANCIENT TOWERS

Mr Haight takes a group of Eton boys – including James – on an expedition to the island. Most interesting is the presence of mysterious dominating towers called the nuraghi. Constructed from huge blocks of basalt, which would have been cut and hauled from extinct volcanoes – no mortar or foundations were used. The only thing keeping the structure together is the immense weight of the stone.

'The tower had stood there for 3,000 years. Built from massive blocks of black stone, some over 6 feet long. How the ancients had got them here and piled them on top of each other, James couldn't imagine. There was something of the ancient mystery of Stonehenge about the place.'

There are more than 7,000 nuraghi of varying sizes to be found all over Sardinia. But even an expert like Mr Haight can only guess at how they were built and the reason for their existence – perhaps the stones had a religious significance or an astronomical meaning, or maybe they were built as fortresses to defend inland areas from invaders. Whatever the reason, historians know that the towers

were built by a mysterious prehistoric civilization that once lived on the island. Not a great deal is known about the Nuraghic people but evidence of their settlements can be found all over Sardinia.

The 'lost' tribe

One Nuraghic tribe is known to have survived right into Roman times, hidden in a valley called the Valley of Lanaittu. Their village was discovered a hundred years ago, and was built within a vast natural cavern inside a mountain – an ideal place to be concealed from enemies. The village can be visited today, although the roof of the cavern has collapsed.

After a few days of Nuraghic investigation, made torturous by the fierce heat, James decides it is time to leave the Eton boys and visit his cousin, Victor Delacroix, who has made his home in Sardinia. Victor lives on the north coast at a spectacular spot called Capo d'Orso – Cape of the Bear – a reference to the nearby rock that resembles a bear on all fours.

Danger in the Waters

During his stay with Victor, James becomes irritated by the fact that Mauro, the houseboy, constantly ignores him. He makes a reckless dive from a high ledge into the sea to impress the Sardinian boy, then triumphantly swims back to shore. But as he wades the last few metres James feels an excruciating pain in his foot.

'Several broken black spines were sticking out of his heel.

He'd trodden on a sea urchin.

There was a terrible burning sensation as the poison, still pumping from its broken spines, soaked into his flesh.'

James has fallen prey to a poisonous sea urchin, a danger that sometimes lurks in the shallow waters of the Sardinian coastline. Mauro tries to help by picking out the spines but the barbed ends remain in James's heel, discharging even more poison when touched. James is in agony but Mauro tries another method. He washes the foot with vinegar, then plunges it into hot water. Grabbing a smooth stone he pounds James's foot hard and continuously. Incredibly painful at first, gradually it seems to work.

'Smashing the spines with a rock breaks down the poison and crushes the tips to dust so that your body can easily deal with them. If the spines are left in they can be the devil.'

Afterwards, James discovers that Mauro's friend Luigi had quite a different idea – he wanted to urinate on James's foot.

How NOT to treat a jellyfish sting

Luigi's suggestion probably stems from the popular idea that weeing on a jellyfish sting will help the pain and make the sting better. This is a myth. In fact, it is probably the worst thing to do if you come into contact with a jellyfish as the urine will aggravate the jellyfish stingers into releasing even more of their poisonous venom.

Fact

SEA URCHINS

The sea urchin is a member of the Echinoderm family, meaning 'spiny skin'. Sea urchins can have long or short spines but all are sharp and can cause injury to humans, though only some types are poisonous. They use poison sacs at their tips of their spines, as well as pincer-like jaws called pedicellaria, to deliver their venom.

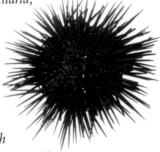

Sea urchins are slow-moving, non-aggressive creatures and, as James discovers, injuries usually happen when a bather or diver accidentally comes into contact with one. Though sea urchin stings are rarely fatal – except possibly in very large numbers – they are extremely painful and the burning, stinging sensation may last for several hours. In severe cases, the victim may also experience nausea, vomiting and even muscular paralysis.

Sardinian Wrestling

When James finds himself at Ugo Carnifex's palazzo in the mountains, he spots a noisy mob of men clustered around some kind of show. He goes over to investigate and sees that Ugo is watching a display of Sardinian wrestling.

'The rules looked simple enough. Men in loose shepherd's outfits grabbed hold of each other and tried to throw their opponent to the ground. As far as James could make out, the loser was the man who bit the dust two times out of three.'

WRESTLING—SARDINIAN STYLE

In Sardinia, wrestling — called *S'Istrumpa* — is a tradition thousands of years old. The wrestlers, or istrumpadores, are local men who challenge each other in this trial of strength and skill. Displays of wrestling may take place at celebrations, weddings, festivals or at organized competitions, and there are annual championships held in the village of Ollalai, situated in the Nuoro province, the heartland of Sardinian wrestling.

WRESTLING RULES
James immediately sees that the rules are very simple.
1. No blows, punches or kicks.
2. The wrestler may grip his opponent's wrists, hands or waist.
3. The winner is the person who forces the other on to the ground in two out of three rounds (or three out of five rounds if the wrestlers are feeling energetic).

When Ugo Carnifex ties James up and threatens to unleash the most deadly animal in the world upon him, images of all kinds of creatures run through James's mind. Then he realizes what Ugo is referring to – a mosquito.

> **'I have known men go mad here as they are covered in a living carpet of mosquitoes, each sticking their long filthy snout under the skin.'**

Ugo is right about the mosquito being deadly. These flying insects may be tiny, but they kill millions of people every year because they spread disease. Mosquitoes exist in many countries of the world but they are particularly rife in Africa, South and Central America and Asia. Over 2,500 different species of mosquito have been identified.

DEADLY DISEASES

'They were flying into his ears, the noise so loud it felt like they were drilling through to his brain.'

The female mosquito needs a meal of blood for her eggs to develop. She detects carbon dioxide, breathed out by living creatures, and makes her landing. She injects saliva to help her feed, then uses her elongated proboscis – a long mouth-like organ – to suck out the blood of the unfortunate creature. During this process she can easily transmit viruses and parasites to the victim without catching anything herself.

One of the most common diseases transmitted via mosquito is malaria. This is carried by a microscopic parasite called plasmodium, passed on in the saliva of the infected mosquito. The parasites multiply in the body's liver, then return to the blood where they break down the red cells. The disease can be fatal. The cycle continues when an infected person is bitten by another mosquito. The insect then picks it up and passes it on to the next victim.

• Ugo takes great pleasure in describing the symptoms of malaria to James – a burning fever, spasms of shivering, pain in the joints and a terrible headache.

• Malaria can be treated with drugs such as quinine and chloroquine but many of the parasites have evolved and are now resistant to most of the drugs in existence.

• *Mosquitoes can also pass on other deadly diseases such as West Nile virus, encephalitis, dengue fever and yellow fever. An outbreak of a tropical virus called chikungunya was recently confirmed in Italy for the first time, caused by mosquitoes. The effect of global warming means that disease-carrying mosquitoes are now much more common in Europe.*

• *A Hebrew text states that the Roman Emperor Titus was punished by God for destroying the temple in Jerusalem. He sent a mosquito*

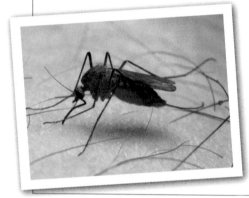

to fly up Titus's nose. It stayed there, picking at his brain and buzzing loudly for seven years until Titus died, crazed by the torture. After his death, they cut open his skull and found a mosquito the size of a bird inside.

The Cars

'She's a fast car, James.
She needs to be driven hard.
Really put your foot down.
You can do it. Just feel the car,
and feel the road ...'

THE CARS

Confidential dossier information

*J*ames is 13 when he first learns to drive. He is taught by his Uncle Max in his black–and–white Bamford and Martin motorcar, with the first lesson taking place in a paddock at the back of Max's house. Uncle Max is a knowledgeable and enthusiastic instructor; in turn, James proves to be an excellent pupil who learns fast and fully appreciates the beauty of a well-constructed vehicle.

When Uncle Max dies, he leaves his beloved car to James, who keeps it hidden in Perry's garage in Windsor. Unknown to the authorities, James occasionally drives the car, and it soon becomes clear that his uncle has bequeathed him a vital skill.

1.5-litre sidevalve short chassis tourer

Description: Powerful open-topped British sports car
Top speed: Known to reach over 135kmph Power: 45hp
First produced: 1923 Number made: Experts estimate 55

Background: In 1913 Robert Bamford and Lionel Martin formed the Bamford and Martin company, selling cars intended for racing and hill-climbing. Soon afterwards they decided to make their own cars and used the name of their favourite driving course at Aston Hill in Buckinghamshire. The legendary Aston Martin company was born.

'Are you going to get out of the way or are you going to die?'

Action: James's two-seater B&M is almost written off by a hysterical Mark Goodenough while speeding on the roads of Windsor. Less than a year later, James is hunted by the violent Smith brothers in a nerve-racking car chase near Cambridge . . .

Background: The Bentley company was founded in Britain in 1919 by Walter Owen Bentley. The supercharged 4.5–litre model was first built in 1929. Also known as the Bentley 'Blower', it is immediately recognizable by the supercharger projecting from under the grille and was once the favourite of British racing drivers.

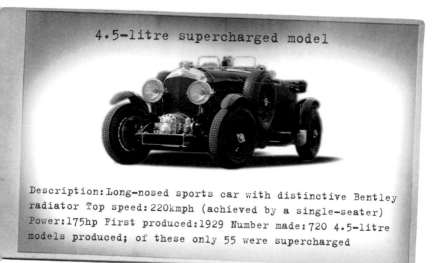

4.5-litre supercharged model

Description: Long-nosed sports car with distinctive Bentley radiator Top speed: 220kmph (achieved by a single-seater) Power: 175hp First produced: 1929 Number made: 720 4.5-litre models produced; of these only 55 were supercharged

'The work was crude and not finished to the usual high standards of Bentley, but somehow it made the car seem more powerful, more rugged. She was a working machine and not a gentleman's plaything.'

Action: Aunt Charmian owns a Bentley 'Blower' and likes nothing more than driving it fast. James vows that he will one day own the same model himself. His wish comes true when he buys a smashed-up Bentley. Restored and modified by the Danger Society, it remains James's proud possession for many years. And twelve years later, we see an adult James Bond driving the very same lovingly restored Bentley.

The Hispano-Suiza Cabriolet

The H6 model

Description: Powerful, luxurious European motorcar
Top speed: Just over 160kmph Power: 90-135hp, depending on model
First produced: 1919 Number made: Many thousands were produced

Background: The Hispano-Suiza company was established in Spain in 1904. During the First World War the company built aircraft engines but returned to car production, making famous models such as the H6 in 1919 and the V12 in 1924. The cars were Swiss-designed but manufactured in France, with engines based on aircraft engine designs.

'James felt alive, all his senses alert. The Hispano-Suiza had a big, powerful engine but he was in control of it.'

Action: In Sardinia, James and local boy Mauro must drive Victor's Hispano-Suiza into the mountains to Ugo's palazzo. The route is treacherous – winding mountain roads, little more than muddy tracks – made all the worse by an exhausted Mauro nodding off at the wheel.

Background: The Daimler company was founded in 1896. The Double Six, so named because of its double six-cylinder unit, also had a powerful V12 engine. The driver of the Daimler was separated from his passengers by an interior wall – harking back to the days when a coach-driver would sit at the front of a horse-drawn carriage.

Description: Large powerful British classic, once favoured by the Royal Family Top speed: 129kmph
Power: 50hp First produced: 1926 Number made: Less than 500

'He laughed silently. Then there was a great whump as the Daimler became a raging ball of fire.'

Action: James is pursued outside Cambridge by a powerful black Daimler, driven by Sir John Charnage's henchmen. A high-speed chase violently forces James's B&M off the road. However, James has his revenge on Charnage . . .

The Dodge Sedan

Background: The Dodge company was founded in the United States in 1900 by brothers Horace and John Dodge. Dodge began making their own cars in 1914, with all-steel body constructions, 12-volt electrical systems and electric starters. Dodge motorcars were extremely well built and known for their dependability.

```
Description:Durable, flat-roofed American classic
Top speed:72kmph Power:35hp First produced:1916
Number made:Unknown
```

'James noticed a small hole in the windscreen. He touched it.

"Yeah," said Manny, and he laughed. A crazy high-pitched laugh, almost like a scream. "That was me. Mama's little boy. Shot a hole right through the windshield. Bam! Driver didn't want to stop. Now, don't you think that was rude?"'

Action: In Mexico, James and Precious are picked up in a black Dodge Sedan driven by a deranged Manny, one of Mrs Glass's gang members. He tells them he has shot the previous driver – a boast borne out by the bullet-hole in the windscreen.

Supercharged Model J

Description: Large, luxurious American car, driven by film stars and royalty Top speed: 217kmph Power: 320 hp First produced: 1932 Number made: Only 11 supercharged models were ever produced

'The car was a beast, frighteningly powerful. James had to struggle to keep it under control.'

Background: The American Duesenberg brothers formed their company in 1913. Their Model J, unveiled in 1928, had two overhead camshafts and contained instruments not often seen in cars at this time, such as a stopwatch and a barometer. The Model SJ came on the market in 1932 with an in-built supercharger next to the engine.

Action: Owned by Jack Stone in Tres Hermanas, Mexico. During a storm, Stone's house is broken into by Mrs Glass and her gang. James drives Stone's children to safety but when the local river bursts its banks, it unleashes a sheer wall of water down upon them. The 'Doozy' is lost to the stormy waters.

James Learns to Drive

'Max ran a hand over the engine. "The noise you hear of an engine roaring," he said, "that's countless small explosions going off, all four cylinders working together, turning that crankshaft."

He slammed the bonnet, straightened up and gripped James by the shoulder. "How would you like to drive her?"'

The 4-stroke engine and how it works

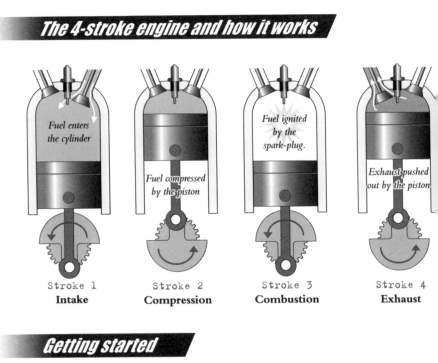

Fuel enters the cylinder

Fuel compressed by the piston

Fuel ignited by the spark-plug.

Exhaust pushed out by the piston

Stroke 1
Intake

Stroke 2
Compression

Stroke 3
Combustion

Stroke 4
Exhaust

Getting started

IMPORTANT: *Learning to drive is a complicated business and beginne MUST be taught by a knowledgeable driver or proper instructor. Beginne must hold a provisional driving license (in Great Britain you need to be 1 before you can learn to drive).*

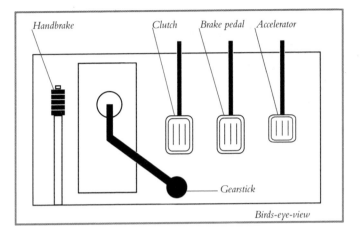

Handbrake   Clutch   Brake pedal   Accelerator

Gearstick

Birds-eye-view

James soon learns all about the workings of the car. At the driver's feet are three foot pedals. From left to right, they are the clutch, the foot brake and the accelerator. The clutch pedal frees the engine to allow a change of gear. The gearstick is beside the left arm and can be moved into different gear positions depending on the speed. There is a handbrake close to the gearstick, which is used to keep the car stationary.

'Starting from scratch and moving off is probably the hardest part. For you and for the car. Picture yourself walking up a steep mountain. To start off, you have to take small, quick, powerful steps, it's a hell of a strain, but coming down the other side, you can take long, slow, easy strides. That's what it's like for a car. To get her moving takes terrific power, but once she's up and running it's much easier. Understand?'

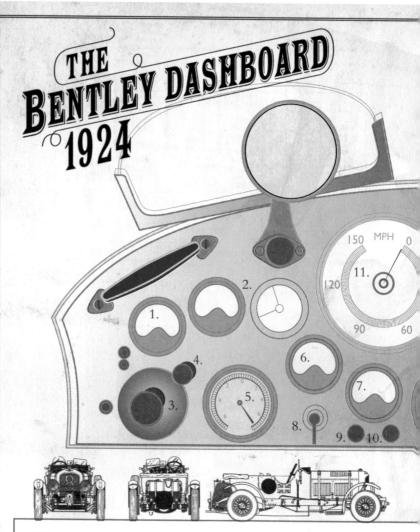

THE BENTLEY DASHBOARD 1924

KEY:

1. Magneto gauges – essential for starting the engine. These gauges show you the temperature of the car's magnetos – devices that supply the engine's spark plugs with the electricity they need.
2. Ammeter – measures the electrical current going to and from the car battery. A flat battery means you're going nowhere.
3. Fuel pump primer
4. Windscreen wipers – a must for rainy days
5. Compressor – shows you the level of air pressure in the system
6. Water temperature – check for overheating
7. Oil temperature
8. Indicator switch – to let others know when you're planning to turn left or right

9. Fog light
10. Lights – switch on as dusk approaches
11. Speedometer – check constantly to make s[ure] you're within the speed limit (a single-seat[ed] Bentley Blower could reach up to 220kmp[h] it would not have been advisable to try this
12. Horn – should only be used as a warning s[ignal] (not to vent anger at other drivers)
13. Ignition control and starting lever – used to the car. Some vintage models had an electr[ic] starter button; others had keys to start the i[gnition] The small light above the lever glows red w[hen] the engine starts.

Driving a car in the 1920s and 30s would have been a very different experience to driving today. Take a look at this Bentley dashboard to see what a driver in James's time would have had to learn about his vehicle.

Tachometer
Measures the revolutions per minute of the engine, showing how fast it is running
Fuel gauge – check to see if the petrol is low and needs filling up
Radiator water pressure gauge
Fuel pressure gauge
Magneto switches
The Bentley has two magnetos (see 1), one for each set of cylinders
Petrol pump
One for each set of cylinders
Electric fan – this cools down the radiator
Fuel close-down from smaller tank

22. Two switches – the left adjusts the timing of the engine. The right is a hand throttle used to help maintain speed. Driving would have been a bumpy experience at this time and it was sometimes hard to keep an even pressure on the foot pedal.
23. Oil pressure gauge
24. Dashboard lights
25. On/off switch for electricity. In an emergency all power can be instantly cut off.

In the Driver's Seat

James finds that starting a car is more difficult than he thought. Here is what he learnt from Uncle Max:

● *To start off, James presses down on the clutch pedal and makes sure the gearstick is in a neutral position.*

● *Then he presses the electric starter to get the engine running (today's cars have keys to start the ignition).*

● *Keeping the clutch pedal down, James puts the car into first gear by moving the gearstick into the first gear position. He applies the foot brake pedal and releases the handbrake. When he's ready to start moving, he gently lets his foot off the brake pedal.*

● *James begins to release the clutch pedal slowly. Placing his foot on the accelerator he pushes down gently as he continues to release the clutch. If it is pushed too hard, the engine will race and growl — too softly and the car won't move off. If James gets it right, the car will slowly move forward.*

"'Not so rough," said Max. "You have to feel the pedals, get just the right balance between the accelerator and the clutch. Too little power, and she won't cope. She'll stall. Too much power, and she'll leap away from you. Think you're ready to have a go?"

"As ready as I'll ever be.'"

Location: London

James returns to Eton after the summer holidays, happy to be a schoolboy again. The routines of school life take over but, just as everything is getting back to normal, one of the Eton teachers, Mr Fairburn, suddenly disappears. To solve the mystery, James and his friends must travel to London. The key landmarks over the page are part of the puzzle.

London is the capital city of England and the United Kingdom *Population:* Approx. 7,556,9000 *Area:* 1,706.8 km². *Languages spoken:* English. However, almost one third of Londoners were born outside the UK and it is estimated that over 250 different languages from all over the world are spoken here. *Flag:*

◉ Originally built as a port on the River Thames, London was founded by the invading Romans 2,000 years ago. They called their city Londinium and it became the capital of Roman Britain. In AD 60 it was burned to the ground by the warrior-queen Boudicca in a violent uprising against the Romans. When the Roman empire crumbled in the fifth century, Angles, Saxons and Jutes arrived from Germany, and the city was later raided by boats full of fierce Vikings who sailed up the Thames.

◉ The city changed hugely between 1066 and 1500 as it grew in importance as a trading centre. Ships would line the banks of the Thames to offload their goods and take more on board for export.

◉ The nineteenth century saw a massive increase in industry, and the building of railways. Thousands of people arrived in London looking for work and between 1801 and 1901 the city's population increased from 1.1 million to 6.6 million. London was now the the buzzing centre of world trade.

◉ The city has suffered much destruction in the past. The Great Fire of London (1666), wiped out two thirds of the city, while many parts of London, including the Houses of Parliament, were damaged or destroyed by the terrifying bombing raids of the Blitz in the Second World War.

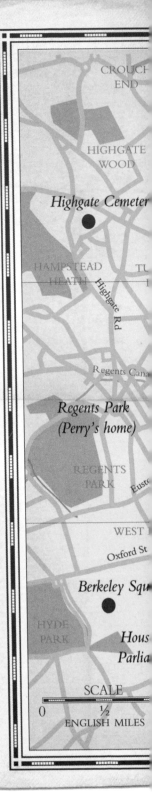

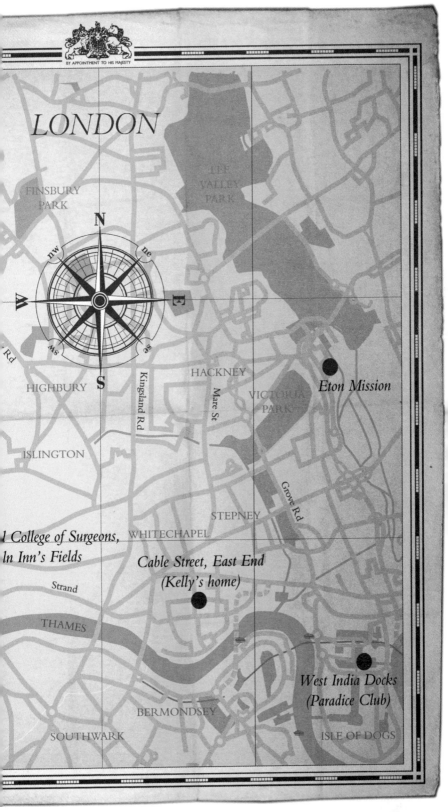

LONDON

FINSBURY
PARK

LEE
VALLEY
PARK

N
nw   ne
W   E
sw   se
S

HIGHBURY

Kingsland Rd

HACKNEY

Mare St

VICTORIA
PARK

Eton Mission

ISLINGTON

Grove Rd

STEPNEY

l College of Surgeons,
In Inn's Fields

WHITECHAPEL

Strand

Cable Street, East End
(Kelly's home)

THAMES

BERMONDSEY

SOUTHWARK

West India Docks
(Paradice Club)

ISLE OF DOGS

. Rd

Life in the East End of London

The East End is an area east of the City of London and north of the River Thames, which includes Hackney, Whitechapel, Mile End, Bethnal Green and Spitalfields. In the nineteenth and early twentieth centuries the East End was one of the poorest areas of the city (unlike the wealthier West End). With its unmade roads, bad drainage and poor housing, the East End was rife with poverty and disease.

'They all looked worn-out and ancient, battered by hard living and poor food.'

It is here that Red Kelly and his family live, in Cable Street. Kelly's father was once a dockworker. In the 1930s, many jobs were temporary and local men would take work at the Thames docks whenever they could get it. The East End was also known for its garment industry, and factories called 'sweat shops' grew up all over the area, offering very hard and badly paid work making clothes. People's biggest fear was to become destitute – with no money to buy food or pay rent – and to end up in the dreaded workhouse.

THE WORKHOUSE

There were workhouses all over the East End but you would have to be desperate to enter one of them. A typical day could involve being set to work breaking rocks with a hammer, with your only food being bread and gruel, a type of thin porridge. Families were split up and children taken away from their parents.

'Growing up in Hackney, in the East End of London, was tough for any kid.'

Despite the poverty, the East End was also known for its sense of community and for its strong family bonds. James can see that the Kelly family are fiercely loyal, and would do anything for a friend. And that includes James.

EAST END COCKNEYS

A Cockney is supposed to be a person 'born within the sound of Bow Bells'. The bells are those of St Mary-le-Bow Church in Cheapside, East London. Cockneys have their own way of speaking and they sometimes use alternative words for everyday things. When Kelly and James meet again, Kelly offers to find him some decent 'clobber' and 'nosh'.

Rhyming slang

Cockneys are famous the world over for occasionally using rhyming slang when they speak. For example:

Apples and pears – stairs
Dog and bone – phone
Barnet fair – hair
Porky pies – lies
Cream crackered – knackered
Tea leaf – thief
Plates of meat – feet
Frog and toad – road

Sometimes the rhyming word is completely left out. So, for example, 'have a butcher's' means 'have a look' (from 'butcher's hook' = look). Or 'use your loaf' means 'use your head' (from 'loaf of bread' = head).

Mr Fairburn's letter to the Crossword Society is full of difficult-to-decipher clues, which appear to show his whereabouts. Eventually James, Pritpal and Perry work out that they are being directed to Highgate Cemetery and the Royal College of Surgeons.

THE GRUESOME MUSEUM

The contents of the museum at the Royal College of Surgeons come as quite a shock to James. And not only to him – during their visit, a boy scout emerges from a lecture and is violently sick. Poor Perry finishes their tour looking rather green too.

'I never want to go back into that chamber of horrors as long as I live.'

What they saw were some of the exhibits at the Royal College of Surgeons' Hunterian Museum (named after the eighteenth-century surgeon and naturalist John Hunter).

The museum traces the history of modern surgery. It houses a jaw-dropping, sometimes shocking, collection of body parts and specimens from natural history. These include the beak of a giant squid brought back from a voyage by Captain Cook, the skeleton of a 2.69-metre-tall Irish giant called Charles Byrne and the diseased bones of an archbishop of Canterbury. There are also foetuses, dissected brains and various body organs – all pickled and floating in jars. (The museum is still open to the public today.)

James finds what the letter is directing him to — specimen D685, the brain of Charles Babbage.

'James peered at the knobbled, pale-grey lumps, swimming in clear liquid.'

He remembers hearing Alan Turing mention Babbage's work when he met him in Cambridge.

THE GREAT BRAIN OF BABBAGE

Charles Babbage was a very clever nineteenth-century inventor who studied mathematics at Cambridge. His great idea was to invent a machine capable of performing calculations much faster than any human. As Pritpal describes, the machine would have been a kind of 'superbrain' into which you could put a problem and get an instant answer.

Babbage believed that you could express all human thoughts as numbers called binary code. He reasoned that if you could do this, then every problem in the universe could be solved. With this great aim, he tried to create two calculating machines, the Difference Engine (1821) and the Analytical Engine (1837). Sadly, his machines couldn't be completed because the technology required was not advanced enough at the time. But he was the earliest computer scientist, the first person to imagine the concept of the computer. His design had many of the logical features of the modern computer — an incredible achievement for its time.

Babbage's Analytical Engine (completed by modern scientists) is on display at the Science Museum in London.

After their grisly experiences with brains and body parts, the boys head north to Highgate Cemetery, where they are looking for the Egyptian tomb referred to in Fairburn's letter. By now it is growing dark and the cemetery is locked. They climb the high wall surrounding it to find an eerie sight within. Wild and overgrown, there are graves and headstones scattered everywhere among the trees and bushes. Even James feels unnerved by the place. His instinct is right. There are real horrors lying within — two brothers who would like to see James dead.

The News.

ONE HALF-PENNY.

HIGHGATE HISTORY

'This whole place is a m-monument to death.'

Situated at the top of Highgate Hill in north London, this famous cemetery was built in 1839 by the Victorians and is full of their favoured Gothic-style tombs and architecture. There are about 167,000 people buried here.

James and Perry are amazed to come upon what looks like an Egyptian temple as they explore the cemetery. This is the Egyptian Avenue with its spectacular arched gateway and lotus-bud columns. There are also two Egyptian-style obelisks, tall four-sided stones with pyramid-shaped tops.

The avenue opens out into the Circle of Lebanon, a sunken walkway containing twenty tombs built around the roots of a dominating cedar tree. The Victorians were very much fascinated by Ancient Egypt, and both cultures shared an obsession with death.

The boys are looking for Nero, and they

eventually find it – a life-size statue of a sleeping lion. Nero was a real lion belonging to George Wombwell, the owner of a travelling menagerie in the nineteenth century. In the days before proper zoos, Wombwell charged the public to see his collection of exotic animals at travelling fairs. He started out with just two boa constrictors and charged a penny per viewing.

Once, at a fair, Wombwell's elephant died and his rival Atkins put up a notice that read 'The Only Live Elephant in the Fair'. Wombwell retaliated with a similar notice saying 'The Only Dead Elephant in the Fair'. Amazingly, his exhibit proved much more popular with the public, who flocked to see the dead body.

FAMOUS RESIDENTS O HIGHGATE

The cemetery is well known for being final resting place of Karl Marx, the fat of communism. Marx was probably most influential political thinker of time. In 1848 he and his colleague Eng wrote a famous pamphlet called T Communist Manifesto, which describ history as a series of class struggl and said that the economic system capitalism would eventually be replace by a new classless and stateless societ His ideas inspired the foundation of man communist regimes in the twentie century and changed the way millions o people live.

Though Marx was German, he settle in London in 1849 and was buried her in 1883. His gravestone is marked by famous and much-visited bust.

On the run from the Smith brothers, James finds himself on Carcass Row, E1, and knows that he is back in the East End. He hears a ship's horn and realizes there must be docks nearby.

But his surroundings are confusing. There is a dark and disused industrial factory close by and James enters it. Much to his surprise, he finds a nightclub. This is the Club Paradice, a smokey, shadowy gambling den.

Fact

GAMBLING DENS

London's docklands used to house many undercover gambling dens and nightclubs. At that time, gambling was illegal in England so these places needed to be hidden away from the police. An outbuilding or old factory in a dark street would have been an ideal location.

Gambling dens were often run by the Chinese, who settled in London in the eighteenth century. Chinese sailors came off the boats at the docks and forged their own Chinatown in Limehouse. There are still lots of Chinese names in the docklands, like Ming Street.

In the Paradice Club James is grabbed by a domineering American, who insists that James helps him to gamble. James doesn't really have much choice, but fortunately he knows a little about the game he is playing from Tommy Chong. It is roulette, the oldest casino game of all.

 Roulette originated in France in 1842, and means 'small wheel'. The object of the game is to pick the winning number on the roulette wheel after it is spun. You can also bet combinations of numbers, choose the colour (red or black) or bet if the number will be odd or even.

 Players do not use cash but buy special roulette chips (tokens) worth varying amounts of money. To avoid disputes, every player receives different colours. To determine the winning number and colour, a croupier (the worker in charge of the table) spins the wheel in one direction, then spins a small silver ball in the opposite direction around the wheel. The ball eventually comes to a halt and falls into one of 37 coloured and numbered pockets on the wheel. The players quickly find out whether they are winners or losers.

If you add up all the numbers displayed on the roulette wheel (from 1 to 36) they total 666 – the number associated with the devil.

Lucky numbers?

Roulette is a game of chance, or luck. And James gets very lucky when he changes his bet at the last moment to his lucky number – seven. The number seven is steeped in superstition and has been regarded throughout history as being a sign of good fortune. The seventh son of a seventh son has magic powers according to Irish folklore; many faiths believe that there are seven heavens; and a seven-sided star, or heptagram, is a traditional symbol for warding off evil (as worn by US sheriffs).

"'Do you trust in my luck or not?" said James.'

The *Girls*

'Wilder wasn't like most of the girls he'd met,
all fussy curls and pretty dresses
that they never wanted to get messy.'

Wilder Lawless

'Wilder Lawless was quite a girl'

Background: Comes from Keithly, in the wilds of the Scottish Highlands. Wilder has grown up with three brothers and can fight as well as any boy.

Appearance: Blonde-haired and pretty, with vivid emerald-green eyes.

Personality: Independent and seemingly fearless.

About Wilder

An animal lover who adores horses, Wilder is often seen riding her beloved Martini.

Many months after meeting her in Scotland, James is amazed to spot Wilder on board the *Colombie*, the liner taking him back to Plymouth from the Caribbean. Wilder has been helping her father transport Argentinian horses across the Atlantic and she is delighted to see James again.

ARGENTINIAN HORSES

"'He's a Criollo," Wilder explained. "A South American breed, descended from horses brought over by the conquistadors. They're clever animals. Very reliable. Very strong.'"

Criollo horses

Horses were introduced to Argentina by the Spanish, who brought the strongest beasts they could find to the Americas. These horses were of the finest Spanish stock but the voyage from Europe was long and hard, and many animals died on the way. The survivors were ridden by the Spanish in violent battles with the native Indians and many of these horses escaped or were driven into the wild.

Over time, herds of hundreds of wild horses became established in the area known as the Pampas, hunted by wild animals and living in a harsh climate that allowed only the fittest to survive. These horses became the forebears of the famous Argentine Criollo breed, one of the strongest, hardiest horses in existence.

Wilder is very proud of her fine Criollo horses and insists on taking James down to the ship's hold to see them. As they view the animals, he remembers how Wilder and her horse, Martini, bravely galloped in to help him during his terrifying pursuit in the Scottish Highlands.

Amy Goodenough

'I've spent half my life on boats.'

Background: The daughter of wealthy English aristocrat Sir Cathal Goodenough and sister of Mark, James's fellow pupil at Eton.

Appearance: Short bobbed hair and pale freckled skin, occasionally mistaken for a boy.

Personality: Brave, defiant, and quick-thinking. Amy is not afraid to fight and she won't put up with any disrespectful behaviour from men.

About Amy

Amy loves the ocean and is an excellent swimmer and sailor. She thinks she is 'the luckiest girl alive' to be going on a sunny sailing holiday with her father, but her luck doesn't hold out for long. Kidnapped by the pirate Zoltan the Magyar, Amy is imprisoned, first on his boat and then in a cell-like room in Sardinia. It is a terrifying time, but Amy remains spirited and defiant. Even her captor begins to admire this courageous young girl.

"'I believe you were sent, Amy," he said. "You are my fate."'

THE KING OF KIDNAPPERS

☀ In the 1960s Sardinia began to get itself a reputation for being a kidnapper's playground. This was due to a group of bandits – among them the notorious Graziano Mesina, Sardina's most well-known bandit – deciding that kidnapping would be much more profitable than their other underhand ventures. The idea had its roots in the bandits' 'traditional' crime of sheep rustling – shepherds would steal sheep from other villages (never their own!) and, over time, this stealing of sheep evolved into actual kidnapping, with wealthy people as the bandits' targets. The bandits also found that the impenetrable landscape of Sardinia, with its many mountains and caves, was the ideal place to keep captives hidden. Kidnapping became a big business for them.

☀ Due to his kidnapping crimes, Graziano Mesina earned himself the dubious name of 'King of Kidnappers'. His other exploits included murder, robbery and jail breaking. But strangely, despite his appalling criminal record, Mesina became a local hero when, while serving a prison sentence in his later years, he helped the authorities arrange the release of a kidnapped 8-year-old boy on the island. He was given a pardon and released from jail.

☀ Whatever people think of him, there's no doubt that Mesina was a daredevil character. First arrested at the age of 14, he spent much of his life (40 years altogether) behind bars. He escaped from the authorities no less than eleven times, once jumping from a moving train while wearing handcuffs, another time jumping out of a third storey window. He even dressed up as a woman in traditional Sardinian costume on one occasion and casually walked out of a building that was completely surrounded by the police.

Vendetta

'Then there was a flash of steel as she whipped out her knife and held it to his throat.'

Background: Comes from a village in the Barbagia region of Sardinia. Younger sister of Mauro, Victor Delacroix's houseboy.

Appearance: Dark tangled hair, brown skin and flashing eyes. Small and lithe, she moves like a cat.

Personality: Has two sides: can be a fearless, savage fighter but also a loving, affectionate companion. Vendetta has fierce emotions and hates disloyalty.

About Vendetta

Raised in a Barbagian village, 13-year-old Vendetta knows the mountains intimately and can walk barefoot on rough terrain without flinching. She also has a streak of terrifying savagery, as James discovers when he sees that she has slit his guard's throat with her sharp blade. The girl is small but deadly.

Vendetta is the product of her hard upbringing. Her name means 'vengeance', in remembrance of a family feud in which her father was killed.

Fact

THE BANDITS OF BARBAGIA

'They are fierce, tough people up there.'

Sardinia's Barbagia region lies inland, and is a hilly, remote area known for its tough bandits. In the past Sardinians would take shelter here from the many invaders that arrived on their shores. The earliest Sardinian bandits were rebellious peasants who saw themselves as fighting against the authority of Rome. In fact, the line between a bandit and a peasant is not clearly defined – Sardinians think of bandits as shepherds who have lost their flocks. Their shepherds have also been described as 'bandits with sheep'. In modern times, bandits have lost their romantic reputation and are better known for robberies and kidnappings.

The law of vendetta

Vendetta's people, the bandits, live by their own rules. They are outlaws – people who literally live 'outside the law' – and their code of honour allows their people to avenge a wrong done to them, or to one of their relatives. This vendetta can carry on for generations and it usually falls to the male who is next of kin to the wronged person to carry out the revenge. In some circumstances, this can take the form of a blood feud – the taking of a life for a life. The family of the victim of revenge is then honour-bound to strike back – and so the vendetta can carry on for generations until sometimes the original cause is completely forgotten. The custom is common to Sardinia and is also known to exist in Corsica and other regions of Italy.

The name 'Barbagia' comes from the Roman statesman Cicero, who described Sardinians as savages because they did not shave as the Romans did (the Latin word for 'beard' is barba). As James discovers, shaving is of little importance for the bandits that he meets.

Kelly Kelly

'I ain't no lady.'

Background: Younger sister of Red Kelly. Lives in the East End of London, one of a large Irish immigrant family.

Appearance: Red-haired like her brother, large brown eyes, a heart-shaped face and a mocking smile.

Personality: Feisty, down-to-earth, good-natured. Loves talking and cracking jokes.

About Kelly

Raised in the rough East End, with a drunk for a dad, Kelly is a tough character. Ringleader of the girl gang The Monstrous Regiment, she is also a fierce fighter. Loyal and full of spirit, Kelly sticks by James throughout his dangerous dockland escapade, and she never lets him down.

THE UNDERGROUND RAILWAY

"'You mean we're going to travel on that thing?" said James.'

Making their way through a dark crypt, Red leads James and Kelly to what looks like a miniature underground station. There is a small carriage shaped like a bullet. This is the pneumatic railway, and luckily for James, it leads directly to an old mail depot at the docks.

'It was impossible to tell how fast they were travelling, but it felt as if they were hurtling along, wildly out of control.'

The pneumatic system uses compressed air to push an object through a tube or tunnel. In the 1800s the engineer William Murdoch used pressurized air to send mail and in 1806 Phineas Balk developed the message cartridge. A cartridge holding documents was loaded into an airtight tube. It was then propelled by compressed air pushing the cartridge or by suction pulling it.

History of the pneumatic system

Pneumatic systems were used mainly in the nineteenth century for transporting small packages across short distances, e.g. within a building or a business. Mail tubes were used to send packages from one location to another. The first was used in 1853. It was 206 metres long and powered by the equivalent of a giant vacuum cleaner.

Experiments were also made with larger systems that could transport bigger cargo underground. The Post Office built a line of underground pneumatic railways in London hoping that high-speed mail deliveries would avoid the traffic overhead. But the scheme proved costly and by 1899 was abandoned.

Plans for the pneumatic railway at Crystal Palace, London, drawn 1864

Precious Stone

'Boys are clumsy and they break things.'

Background: Daughter of American pilot, Jack Stone. Lives in the town of Tres Hermanas, Mexico, with her younger brother, JJ.

Appearance: Dark-eyed with dark hair, waved in a fashionable style. Fancily dressed and made up.

Personality: Seems unfriendly, rude and incredibly spoilt – but is tougher and braver than she first appears.

About Precious

James and Precious's first meeting is not a success. James has never met anyone so superior and insulting but he tries to keep his cool.

After the Stone house is broken into by an armed gang, James, Precious and JJ have to make a long, hard journey in the aftermath of a violent hurricane, during which they face kidnap, violence and injury. And Precious's resources of strength, ingenuity and bravery are tested to the absolute limit when she and James eventually face the horror of El Huracán's rat run.

AN UNWELCOME VISITOR

During the pair's stay on El Huracán's island, James notices a painful-looking insect bite on his shoulder. To his horror he discovers that there is a kind of grub called a botfly growing inside it. The doctor's advice is surprising. He tells James to tape a piece of raw bacon over the bite. The maggot will then burrow upwards into the meat to try to reach its air source.

'James ripped off the bandage and carefully peeled back the strip of blackened bacon beneath it. There was the white head of the grub, nestling in a hole in the flesh.'

Precious delightedly squeezes out the grub and flicks it into the sand where a passing crab gobbles it up.

The human botfly

Dermatobia hominis, *more commonly known as the botfly is a parasite that usually lives on rodents and cattle, but occasionally infests a human. It lives in Mexico and other parts of central and south America.*

The life-cycle begins with an egg-laden female botfly. She captures a mosquito and glues her eggs on to its proboscis – the long feeding organ the mosquito uses to suck blood. When the mosquito bites, it leaves the tiny egg behind in the skin and body heat helps the egg to hatch. A larva begins to grow under the skin. It will increase in size for up to eight weeks – growing up to 25mm long – before leaving in order to pupate into an adult fly.

Roan Power

'You're growing up, James. You're finding out things aren't as simple as you thought.'

Background: Born into a large family in a village in County Tipperary, Ireland. Works as a maid at Eton College but has a secret identity.

Appearance: Startlingly pretty with wavy black hair, white skin and dark shining eyes. A slightly mocking smile.

Personality: Charismatic and charming, but also fiery and headstrong. Roan seems to know a lot about the world and has very strong opinions.

About Roan

When James bumps into Roan at Eton he is immediately attracted by her warmth, prettiness and easy humour. The pair become friends, but James senses that Roan is holding something back. His suspicions are proved right when Roan admits she is torn between her communist beliefs and her personal feelings.

'... sometimes we have to sacrifice the things we love for the greater good.'

WHAT IS COMMUNISM?

In theory, a communist society is a classless society where all private ownership is abolished and where all people enjoy completely equal status.

As a political movement, communism has aimed to overthrow capitalism through a revolution of the workers. Marx and Engels made these ideas popular in their famous 1848 pamphlet The Communist Manifesto, *and Lenin, the first communist ruler of Russia, was inspired by their work. Many nations have been run by communist parties in the twentieth century, e.g. Russia (later known as the Soviet Union), The People's Republic of China, Afghanistan and Cuba.*

Becoming a communist agent

Throughout the 1920s and 30s the Soviet Union actively looked for recruits in Great Britain. They found potential communist agents among groups of young intellectuals, people who were interested in politics and who wanted to play a part in changing the world. Many of these people were worried about the state of the world – in the early 1930s the Great Depression was causing poverty and misery and the Fascist movement was growing in Germany and Italy. The Soviet Union seemed to be the only country strong enough to stand up to the Fascists and its Marxist ideals of equality attracted many to the communist cause.

Roan became involved with communism and left home at 16 to travel all over Europe with the rebellious Dandy. For two years they mixed with artists, thinkers and revolutionaries, discussing the state of the world and coming to the conclusion that communism offered people a better way of living than the capitalist system, in which society is divided into the haves and have-nots.

'We went to secret meetings, we studied books and pamphlets, we learned how the world really turns.'

Real-life communist agents

The Russian intelligence service used Russians, foreign-born nationals and communist-inclined foreigners to perform espionage from the 1920s. Potential agents would usually be recruited via a cell – a small group of agents acting within the larger organization. The agents would often be given code-names as a cover. (Wrangel, for instance, is known as 'Amethyst'.) Their aim was to subvert governments and promote the communist cause.

British intelligence focused their efforts on investigating communist espionage within the armed services and the general public. They exposed a number of Soviet spy rings during the 1920s and 1930s.

Real-life communist agents

Melita Norwood was 25 when she was recruited by the Russians in 1937. She was a British woman who spied for Moscow for more than 40 years under her code-name 'Hola'. Working as a personal assistant for an association that was helping to develop Britain's first nuclear bomb, Melita had access to many important documents, which she supplied to Russian agents during secret meetings. This information helped the Russians develop their own nuclear bomb. It is believed that Melita saved them five years of research time, enabling the Russians to explode their first nuclear bomb in 1949, three years before Britain. This had a huge impact on the balance of power in the world. Melita wasn't exposed until the age of 87, by which time she was a great-grandmother living in south London.

*F*ollowing James's escapades in London, it is decided that he should accompany his Aunt Charmian on her forthcoming trip to Mexico, rather than going straight back to Eton. Docking in Vera Cruz, the pair take a train to Mexico City, and continue to Tampico where Charmian finds a local man to lead her expedition into the rainforest. She leaves James in the care of an American family, the Stones, in the coastal village of Tres Hermanas.

Mexico is a large, highly populated country that borders the United States in the south. It has a varied climate that includes hot deserts, forests and tropical rainforests. Its capital is one of the largest cities in the world.

Capital city: Mexico City Population: Approx. 107 million
Area: 1.9 million km². Languages spoken: Mainly Spanish
speaking, but many indigenous languages are
also spoken.
                                          Flag:

MEXICO

Short History

One of Mexico's earliest peoples, the Olmecs settled on the Gulf coast near Veracruz (spelled 'Vera Cruz' at the time of James's visit) from about 1400 BC, building cities and creating huge stone head carvings. The Olmecs mysteriously vanished around 400 BC, and were succeeded by other ancient peoples, among them the Zapotecs, the Maya and the Aztecs. All were complex civilizations that built cities and had an impressive knowledge of mathematics, astronomy, architecture and other subjects.

The Spanish Conquistadores started to arrive on Mexican shores in 1519, and defeated the Aztecs, taking their gold. Spain then ruled Mexico for nearly 300 years before an uprising ended their reign in 1821.

Later, a time of political turmoil followed, Texas declared its independence from Mexico in 1836 and battles were fought between Mexicans and Texans at the Alamo and San Jacinto. A two-year war with the United States ended in 1848, with Mexico losing a large amount of land to the US. Then, an opportunistic invasion by Napoleon III's army in 1862 lasted until French troops withdrew in 1866. In 1910 Mexican citizens rose up against their presidency in the Mexican Revolution and a new constitution for the country was adopted in 1917.

A Hurricane Hits

When James and Aunt Charmian arrive at the Stones' palatial home, there are clear signs of a storm building up in the Gulf. James, Precious and her brother JJ are left in the house and witness a full-scale hurricane erupt.

'He was mesmerized by the awesome power of the storm. A set of garden furniture rolled across the lawn and knocked over a statue. A large tree near the road, unable to bend, snapped in half and collapsed on to the perimeter wall, flattening it.'

Fact

WHAT IS A HURRICANE?

A hurricane is a huge storm with strong winds blowing at a speed of more than 120 kilometres per hour. A hurricane can form only in certain conditions. It has to form over warm sea (more than 26.5°C) and in areas near the equator. The heat and moisture from the tropical water provides the hurricane's source of energy, and a wind forms over the ocean. The wind begins to spin because of the 'Coriolis Force', an effect of the Earth's rotation.

Hurricanes rotate like spinning tops around a central 'eye', which is the calmest part. When a hurricane spins its way inland it can wreak devastation, washing away roads and bridges, toppling trees and power lines and wrecking homes.

The worst hurricane ever to hit Mexico was in 1959 – Hurricane Mexico. The violent storm caused a huge mudslide in the hills, killing hundreds of people. Many poisonous scorpions and snakes were uncovered in the mud, which posed another threat to people's lives. This hurricane reached Category 5 on the Saffir-Simpson scale, a rare event. Altogether, 1,000 people died.

James and Precious end up walking in the open Mexican scrubland in the heat of the midday sun. Hot, tired and hungry, James needs to find a way of surviving and he sees his chance when a large lizard squats close by. James shoots it, skins it, then cooks it over an open fire. Even the squeamish Precious can't resist devouring the finished results.

'Once the lizard was done, he peeled off the crisp skin with his knife and cut the animal up into pieces. It looked like any plate of meat now, and when he tasted it, it was not unlike a tough chicken. It felt good to have some warm meat inside him.'

SURVIVAL IN THE MEXICAN DESERT

Much of Mexico is covered by deserts, the biggest being the Chihuahuan Desert in the north. This is the largest desert in North America, and despite the extreme climate, there are a huge number of creatures that live here. There are wolves, lions, prairie dogs, foxes and deer as well as many species of insects, birds and reptiles.

Desert temperatures can vary wildly. It can be fiercely hot during the daytime, dropping to bitter sub-zero temperatures at night. During the day, if you don't have enough water to drink, you will suffer from dehydration and the hot sun can cause heatstroke or hyperthermia. This is when the body temperature rises too high, and it can prove fatal. In complete contrast, if you are not warmly clothed in the cold desert night you may suffer from hypothermia – a dangerous cooling-down of the body. This can also be fatal. To avoid hypothermia, put on any extra clothing you have with you, before you start shivering. If possible, build a fire and try to find shelter.

SURVIVING THE HEAT

- Don't sit or lie on the ground, as it is the hottest place. Sit on something like a rock, which is raised higher than the ground.
- If you have water, drink it. Ration your sweat, not water.
- Breathe through your nose and keep your mouth shut to reduce water loss for as long as possible. Suck on a pebble to keep your mouth moist and to reduce the sensation of thirst.

FINDING WATER IN THE DESERT

The human body cannot survive for much more than three days without water.

- All plants need water to survive so there is a chance of finding moisture nearby. Dig down under a plant to see if the ground is damp. If you find damp sand, keep scooping out a hole until water begins to seep into it. If there isn't enough to drink, use your shirt to sponge up whatever you can and squeeze it into your mouth. Just before sunrise is a good time to gather up water from plants which will have dew on them. Again, use your shirt to soak up the moisture and squeeze it out to drink.

There are sometimes water sources under the surface of the ground where water has been retained by layers of rock. Look for ravines or hollows between hills or in the bottoms of canyons in mountainous deserts.

Certain species of cactus contain liquid, but some can also be poisonous so you will need to identify the cactus first. The barrel cactus can be cut open to get to the pulpy inside, where the water can be sucked out from the pulp. It has pink or red thorns that are curved like fish hooks.

Water holes may be found where flocks of birds are circling. Watch and listen for birds, especially in the morning and evening.

Fact

THE STINGING SCORPION

Scorpions are eight-legged venomous creatures related to spiders, mites and ticks. They have a crablike appearance with large pincers and a long segmented tail that curls up, with a notorious stinger at the end (called a telson). Scorpions are extremely hardy creatures and can survive the harshest environments. Scientists have experimented by freezing scorpions overnight, then putting them in the sun the next day. The scorpions simply thaw out and walk away.

There are almost 2,000 scorpion species, but only 30 or 40 have poison strong enough to kill a human. However, all scorpions can inflict a nasty sting. They usually eat insects and spiders, but larger scorpions may attack small lizards, snakes and mice. They lie in wait to ambush their prey, using their strong pincers to grab and hold them. If necessary, they will also paralyse them with their sting.

Symptoms of a scorpion sting

- ☠ Pain or burning sensation at the sting area
- ☠ Sweating, nausea and vomiting
- ☠ Numbness
- ☠ Muscle twitching
- ☠ Heart palpitations
- ☠ Breathing difficulties

If you are stung

If a sting is not serious, clean and dry the area and lie down, keeping the area of the sting at heart level (using pillows for arms and legs). Relieve the pain with an ice pack. Watch out for the symptoms described and go to the hospital if you are worried. Try to capture the scorpion in a lidded container so that you can take it to the hospital with you — they may be able to identify the species to see if it is dangerous for humans.

Advance of the Army Ants

After being captured by Mrs Glass and her henchmen, James and Precious make a desperate break for the jungle. Chased by an angry gun-toting Strabo, they soon run into trouble of a different kind. Nothing can prepare James for the sight he sees when he climbs a tree trunk to see if he can spot their pursuer:

'There must have been a million of them and nothing could stop them. Spiders, scorpions, lizards, even a snake, were struggling to escape, but sinking under a boiling, seething mass of black bodies and red heads with huge slicing mandibles. The ants latched on to anything they could hold – a leg, a wing casing, an antenna, an eye – and after paralysing their prey with their bites they cut them into pieces.'

James has seen his first army ants.

Fact

AN ARMY OF MARCHING STOMACHS

There are many species of army, or soldier, ant but all display similar behaviour. Huge numbers of carnivorous army ants will gather together in aggressive foraging groups to attack their prey. They form columns of as many as 20 million ants, consuming vast numbers of tarantulas, scorpions, beetles, grasshoppers, snakes, lizards, frogs and any other small creatures who get in their way. The ants use their powerful scissor-like jaws, or mandibles, for biting, crushing and cutting. Incredibly, all worker ants are blind, and they use their antennae to follow chemical trails when finding their way around.

The bite of the army ant is very painful, and it is extremely difficult to remove one that has got its strong jaws into you. One of the Masai tribes of East Africa have made effective use of this strength. If suffering a wound while out in the bush they will sometimes use an ant as emergency stitching. This involves picking up an ant and letting it bite on both sides of the wound, then breaking off the ant's body. The jaws that are left behind will hold the wound together for several days.

The Ancient Maya

The villain El Huracán owns the private island of Lagrimas Negras, which lies between the Yucatán Peninsula and the Cayman Islands. The first settlers here were the ancient Maya who built temples, tombs, two pyramids, an observatory and a ball court. A proud El Huracán shows James around the ball court and explains how the Maya used it.

"For the Mayans," said El Huracán, settling down on the stepped seating that surrounded the court, "the aim of warfare was not to kill men but to capture them. The greatest warrior was the one

who could catch the most enemies. The prisoners would then be brought back to the city and taken to the temple, where they would have their living heart torn out of their chests by a priest, as an offering to the ever-hungry gods.

"The ball game was a religious ceremony played in their honour. There were games at every religious event. Sometimes the players would be captured slaves, but not always.'"

The ball game was taken very seriously by the Mayan people, and particularly by those who played it. The losing team, or the team's leader, would very often be beheaded. For the Maya there was no clear line between sport and war.

HOW TO PLAY AT THE MAYAN BALL COURT
Almost every Mayan city had its own ball court. The Great Ball Court at Chichén Itzá in Mexico is the largest ball court in the world, measuring 166 by 68 metres. In these times the ball game was called pitz.

THE RULES
- Players are not allowed to use their hands or feet to touch the ball. They must use their hips, chests, shoulders and knees.
- The ball must be kept moving at all times.
- Players must try to get the ball through stone hoops set high up on the walls. Players are allowed to wear protective padding.

As you can imagine, trying to knock a ball upwards through a high hoop without using your hands or feet would have been very difficult. Especially as the rubber ball used was a heavy one — roughly 20cm in diameter and weighing between 3-4kg. It would have been 15 times heavier than the average volleyball.

The leader of the winning side would be honoured and awarded feathers. Meanwhile the losers could only hope for a swift death and a happy afterlife.

THE LEGEND OF THE HERO TWINS

The ball game is believed to play out the Mayan myth of the Hero Twins. In the story, the twins, Xbalanque and Hunahpu, had to battle the gods of death by playing a ball game with them.

Before the game began, the twins were subjected to series of ordeals in different houses, but managed to survive most of them through wit and cunning — for example, in the Jaguar House, the twins distract the animals by feeding them bones. However, in the B House, Hunahpu's head gets cut off, but in the sto he continues with his head replaced by a squash.

According to the myth, the twins eventually win the game and they rise into the heavens to become the s and the moon. The ball used in the game is belie to represent the sun moving across the sky.

El Huracán is keeping a horrible secret from James and Precious – his infamous rat run, *La Avenida de la Muerte*. Set in an ancient Mayan pyramid, it is a series of interlinked passageways in which lurk unimaginable horrors. The victim must act out a Mayan belief: making the descent into Xibalba, the legendary Realm of the Dead, and being forced along a road of treacherous obstacles.

Gods of the Maya

The Maya believed in many gods and goddesses, around 190 altogether. They had gods to represent many different things, from the sun and rain to suicide and death.

Chac – the rain god was a benevolent god whom the Maya often turned to for help in growing crops. He was associated with the creation of life.

Yum Cimil – the death god, head of the underworld Xibalba. His body is mostly skeleton and he wears adornments made of bones.

Hurakan – god of wind, storm and fire, also associated with the creation of life. He made a great flood in the world when the humans angered the gods.

'He glanced back to see the huge, dark shape sliding
slowly off the ledge into the water. He thought he might
be sick with fear. He wasn't going to make it in time.'

Crossing the Atlantic

To thank James for helping Precious and JJ, their father arranges a treat for him – a week's island-hopping in the Caribbean on board a luxury yacht. When it is time to return to England, James and his aunt sail for Pointe-à-Pitre, the port on the island of Grande Terre. Here they board the *Colombie*, the French liner that will take them back across the Atlantic to England.

THE STEAMSHIP

The *Colombie* is an impressive sight, nearly 150 metres long and able to carry 500 passengers. The ship is owned by the Compagnie Générale Transatlantique fleet, also known as the French Line.

The French Line was founded in 1861 and became renowned in the early twentieth century for its luxurious liners. Its most famous liner was the *Normandie*, which operated in the 1930s. She could carry 1,975 passengers and 1,345 crew and was the largest ship in the world at the time of her completion. She was also the fastest.

The Blue Riband was an award given for the fastest Atlantic crossing and many liners in the early twentieth century competed to win it. The *Normandie* earned it when she made the journey in four days. Previously, the liner *Mauretania* had been the longest holder of the Blue Riband, from 1907 to 1929. She could reach a top speed of 50 kilometres per hour and made 538 Atlantic crossings in her lifetime.

Steamship history

Until the nineteenth century, journeys by sea were slow and uncomfortable as ships relied on the wind to power their sails. With the advent of steam power, a new type of ship came into use, pioneered by the British engineer Isambard Kingdom Brunel. The early steamships had sails to assist the engines but by the late nineteenth century steamships were becoming bigger and faster. Special ships were built to carry passengers across the Atlantic and the Pacific, called liners because they sailed regular routes or lines. The liners offered passengers a much faster and more reliable service and were also used to transport cargo and mail. The golden age of the liner was in the 1920s and 30s when their popularity and use were at their peak.

The big steamship companies, such as Cunard, realized they could make money out of the many people who wanted to emigrate. At the end of the nineteenth century and beginning of the twentieth, thousands of people left their homes in Europe to try to make a better life for themselves in countries like the United States, Canada and South Africa. They sailed the Atlantic on huge liners but could often only afford the very cheapest tickets. These dark, smelly and overcrowded dormitories on the lower decks were called steerage. First-class passengers, however, had a very different experience on the upper decks, staying in elegant private cabins with all their needs attended to.

The most famous liner

One of the most famous steamships ever is the *Titanic*, the luxury liner that set out on its maiden voyage in 1912. It carried 2,227 passengers and crew from Southampton, in England, and was headed for New York City. The ship was said to be unsinkable but on the night of 14 April, it hit a huge iceberg and sank. There were only 705 survivors.

The Weapons

'MacSawney grinned and fired at James.
The bullet ricocheted off the wall,
two inches from his head.'

THE WEAPONS

Confidential dossier information

*T*aking part in the Hellebore Cup shooting event gives James his first experience of holding a gun – a .22 Browning rifle, to be exact. He turns out to be an excellent shot. But it isn't long before James finds himself on the other end of a weapon.

'With a flourish like a cheap magician, Meatpacker rolled up a trouser leg and displayed a small, pearl-handled revolver strapped to his shin in a leather holster.

"Is that a Derringer?" asked Kelly.

"It sure is."

Kelly laughed. "I thought that was a lady's gun."

"Well, now, and aren't I a lady's man?" said Meatpacker, and he laughed his great booming laugh again.'

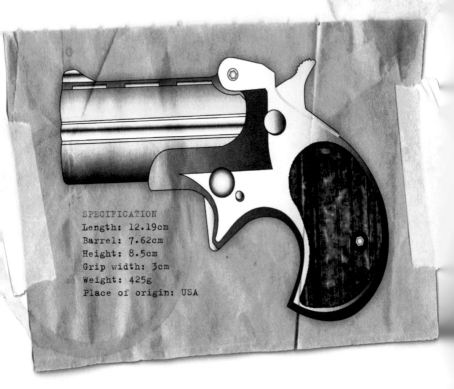

SPECIFICATION
Length: 12.19cm
Barrel: 7.62cm
Height: 8.5cm
Grip width: 3cm
Weight: 425g
Place of origin: USA

> **IMPORTANT:** *Guns are extremely dangerous and the UK has very strict gun laws. These laws are there to prevent misuse of guns and potential harm to the public. There are severe penalties for anyone who breaks these laws.*

The History

- Named after Henry Deringer, the American gunsmith who invented them, Deringer pistols were sold from the 1860s to the 1930s. The misspelled word 'Derringer' also became a generic name for any small pocket pistol of a similar design.

- The Derringer was a small weapon with a very short barrel, making it easy to conceal. It became popular with those who wanted to keep their weapon out of sight – private detectives included. Derringers also had a reputation for being ladies' guns because they could be kept in a handbag or concealed in a stocking-top. However, the barrel size meant that Derringers were not particularly accurate when fired, unless used at very close range.

- John Wilkes Booth used a Derringer pistol to assassinate President Lincoln in 1865 at Ford's Theatre in Washington. Booth dropped the gun while making his getaway and the pistol can be seen today in the Ford's Theatre Museum.

Brothers Wolfgang and Ludwig Smith are ruthless thugs who will do any kind of unpleasant job – even murder – if the price is right. And to perform this dirty work, Ludwig has had two horribly inventive weapons adapted for himself – Apache revolvers. He first heard about this multi-purpose weapon in Paris, where he became fascinated by its violent history.

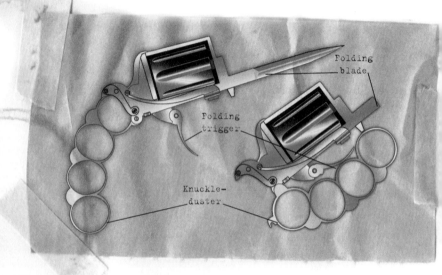

'He was holding two weird and sinister weapons – stubby revolvers, with very short muzzles, whose grips were knuckledusters.

Ludwig smiled. His hands were not shaking. They were rock solid. As he raised the guns towards the boys a narrow bayonet slid out of the end of each weapon with a metallic click and snapped into place. The blades were not much thicker than knitting needles and tapered to tiny stiletto points.'

- The Apache is a compact, multi-purpose weapon comprising a revolver, a knuckleduster and a small fold-out dagger. The knuckleduster also functions as the grip of the weapon. The 7mm calibre revolver uses a pinfire method of ignition, in which a hammer strikes a pin to set it off.

- The revolver is named after the notorious French Apache gangs, who operated in the streets of Paris in the late 1800s and early 1900s. They were said to have created the weapons for use in their criminal activities. The gangs gained their name when their savagery was compared to that attributed by Europeans to the native Apache tribes of North America.

- Since the Apache revolver had no barrel, its range was limited. But as it measured little more than four centimetres across when folded, it had the advantage of being easily concealed while out on the streets. It was a frightening-looking device that would have helped the Apache gangs promote a culture of fear.

- British commandos during the Second World War used a multi-purpose revolver of a similar design to the Apache.

The Goodenough family's Mediterranean sailing holiday is rudely interrupted when the villainous Zoltan and his henchmen arrive by boat and take over their vessel. The pirates soon make their intentions clear. They are after Sir Cathal's precious bronze statuette – and they have enough weapons at their disposal to do whatever they like.

'Goodenough recognized the pistol: it was an Italian navy-issue 9-millimetre Beretta. These men were no scruffy, disorganized opportunists: they were serious professionals.'

SPECIFICATION
Length: 21.6cm
Barrel: 12.45cm
Cartridge: 9x19mm
Parabellum weight: 950g
Place of origin: Italy

Zoltan switches between his Beretta and a machine gun, but, as he informs James, he prefers the pistol.

'She is small and has no great stopping power, but I like her. She suits me; she is fast and reliable and I can hide her easily.'

The History

● The Italian Beretta company is one of the oldest manufacturing firms in the world, with a history of making firearms that dates back to 1526. The early twentieth century was a time of growth for Beretta, who developed their first pistol during the First World War – the Model 1915. It had a relatively simple and compact design with a fixed barrel and blowback operation. This system uses the pressure created by combustion in the cartridge case and bore to reload the gun.

● Beretta are also famous for their Model 1934, a semi-automatic (self-loading) blowback pistol designed specifically for use by the Italian military. Made with few parts and simple to maintain, its durability meant it could have a life of more than 100 years.

● The Beretta 1934 was used extensively during the Second World War and was 'liberated' in significant numbers from Italian armed forces by Allied soldiers, who liked its compactness.

The Thompson Sub-Machine Gun

Zoltan supplies the power-crazy Ugo Carnifex with a crate of Thompson sub-machine guns.

'So simple and so deadly.'

Drum magazine

SPECIFICATION
Length: 85cm
Weight: 4.9kg
Rate of fire: 600-1200rpm
 depending on model
Designer: John Taliaferro Thompson
Place of origin: USA

- The Thompson sub-machine gun – or 'tommy gun' – was invented by American John T. Thompson during the First World War. He wanted to design a weapon that was lightweight, portable and that could be used on the move. The tommy gun weighed less than a quarter of existing machine guns yet had the same firepower as larger models.

- The gun had a distinctive circular magazine that carried up to a hundred rounds of ammunition. The bolt flicked out the spent cartridge while the spring-loaded magazine loaded a new one.

- Thompson described his invention as a 'trench broom', for 'clearing' men out of trenches. The First World War was characterized by trench warfare. Initially, soldiers dug trenches as a short-term defensive measure but ended up living in them and fighting from them for almost the whole of the war.

- After the war, the tommy gun became the weapon of choice for American gangsters of the 1920s and 30s, such as the notorious Al Capone. In the infamous St Valentine's Day Massacre of 1929, when Capone had members of the rival 'Bugs' Moran gang 'rubbed out', two tommy guns did most of the erasing. In 1934 the US government passed the National Firearms Act in an attempt to limit the use of these dangerous guns.

The Enfield Revolver

It is highly appropriate that the gun James finds and uses when escaping from Baron von Schlick's castle is a British one – the Enfield Number 2 Mark I.

'He tested the firing mechanism, pulling the trigger four times. It all worked smoothly. Carefully he reloaded it. It was heavy in his hand. He would have to make sure he held it securely when the time came because he would only have the chance to make one shot.'

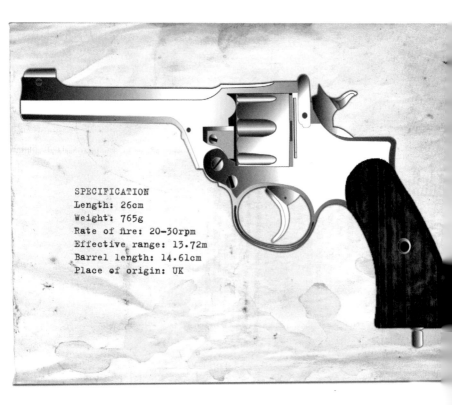

```
SPECIFICATION
Length: 26cm
Weight: 765g
Rate of fire: 20-30rpm
Effective range: 13.72m
Barrel length: 14.61cm
Place of origin: UK
```

The Enfield revolver was a British handgun manufactured by the government's Royal Small Arms Factory in Enfield. It was developed as a replacement for the Webley Mark VI in the 1920s. The Number 2 Mark I revolver was produced from 1923 to 1957 and was one of the standard sidearms used by the British and Commonwealth army throughout the Second World War.

The Enfield was a double-action revolver with a six-chamber cylinder. The original model had a hammer spur, but the later Number 2 Mark I model had the spur removed. This made the gun easier to draw (no snagging) and easier to conceal. However, the spur's removal did have an effect on the revolver's accuracy – hence the statement by one of the villains:

'The Enfield is notoriously inaccurate at distance.'

Despite this opinion, the Number 2 Mark I was just as accurate as similar handguns of its time. It was also fast to shoot because of its relatively light double-action trigger pull, while its automatic ejector, which removed all six cases from the cylinder simultaneously, made it quick to reload.

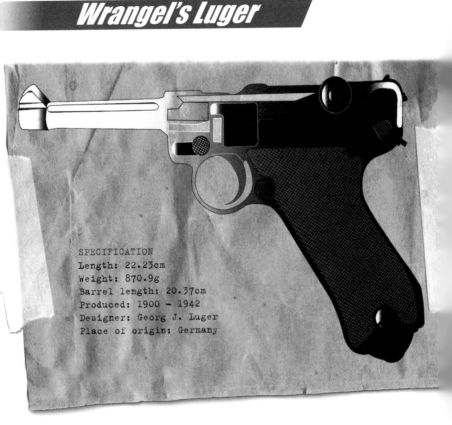

SPECIFICATION
Length: 22.23cm
Weight: 870.9g
Barrel length: 20.37cm
Produced: 1900 - 1942
Designer: Georg J. Luger
Place of origin: Germany

The Luger is the favoured weapon of sinister puffy-eyed Russian Vladimir Wrangel.

'Wrangel has a superior weapon, and is an excellent marksman and, what is more, he has successfully killed several men with his Luger. I wonder, James Bond, how many men you have killed?'

- Georg Luger patented the Parabellum-Pistole – otherwise known as the Luger – in 1898, though his design was based on an earlier model by Hugo Borchardt. Lugers were produced from 1900 by German arms manufacturer DWM and they became the standard German sidearm during the First World War. They were also used in the Second World War.

- The Luger is a semi-automatic magazine-fed pistol that operates on a short-recoil principle. Its most distinctive feature is its toggle-lock action, which uses a jointed mechanism, rather like the joint of a knee. Other semi-automatic pistols usually have a slide action.

How a modern pistol works

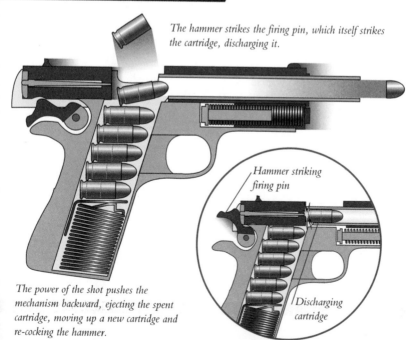

The hammer strikes the firing pin, which itself strikes the cartridge, discharging it.

Hammer striking firing pin

Discharging cartridge

The power of the shot pushes the mechanism backward, ejecting the spent cartridge, moving up a new cartridge and re-cocking the hammer.

The Body as a Weapon

There are many other deadly weapons that are used against James during his hair-raising adventures. But one of the most challenging adversaries he meets is a man who uses not a gun or a knife but his body as a lethal weapon. Japanese Sakata is a master of ju-jitsu and can fell a man in one skilled and elegant move.

About Ju-Jitsu

The word 'ju-jitsu' literally means 'gentle art' or 'art of softness'. This martial art emphasizes the principle of using the attacker's own force against him or herself. It originally evolved among the samurai warriors of Japan as a way of defeating an armed opponent without weapons and while using the least amount of force necessary.

A ju-jitsu pupil learns how to evade attack and how to assess the force of an attack in order to use that energy against the perpetrator. He or she will also learn how to target the various nerves and pressure points of the attacker.

'James lunged, and again Sakata was ready for him. Quick as a cat, he grabbed James's wrist and turned him. There was an excruciating pain in his elbow. He dropped the knife and the next thing he knew he was flat on his back with Sakata standing over him, still holding his arm in a lock.'

There are many moves and positions in ju-jitsu. These usually take the forms of pins, joint locks and throws. Some of the names for these moves include:

FORWARD ROLL
BACK-HAMMER LOCK
STRAIGHT ARM LOCK
CRAB CLAW SCISSORS THROW
ESCAPE FROM BEAR HUGS

柔

術

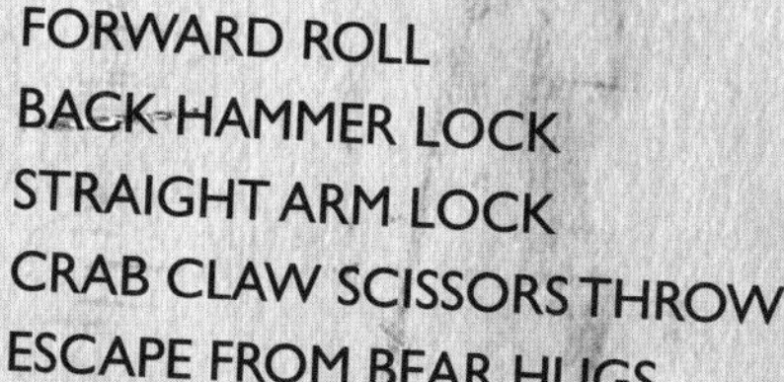

Other martial arts, such as judo, have developed from ju-jitsu.

Before tackling ju-jitsu, James learnt to defend himself through the sport of boxing. As one would expect, he is fast on his feet and has a good strong punch.

'James nipped in and gave him a quick jab to the side of his undefended belly and Fitzpaine swore, launching a wild punch at James's head. The glove glanced off the side of James's face. It should have been fairly harmless, but James felt his whole head jar and he tasted blood in his mouth.

Hell.

Fitzpaine's punch was harder than it looked.'

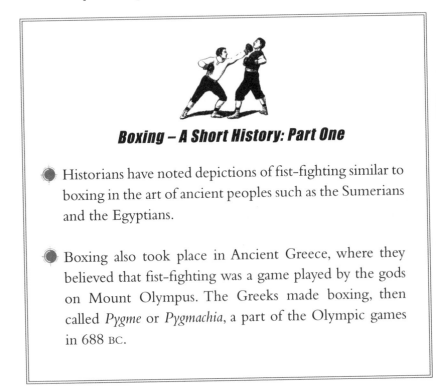

Boxing – A Short History: Part One

- Historians have noted depictions of fist-fighting similar to boxing in the art of ancient peoples such as the Sumerians and the Egyptians.

- Boxing also took place in Ancient Greece, where they believed that fist-fighting was a game played by the gods on Mount Olympus. The Greeks made boxing, then called *Pygme* or *Pygmachia*, a part of the Olympic games in 688 BC.

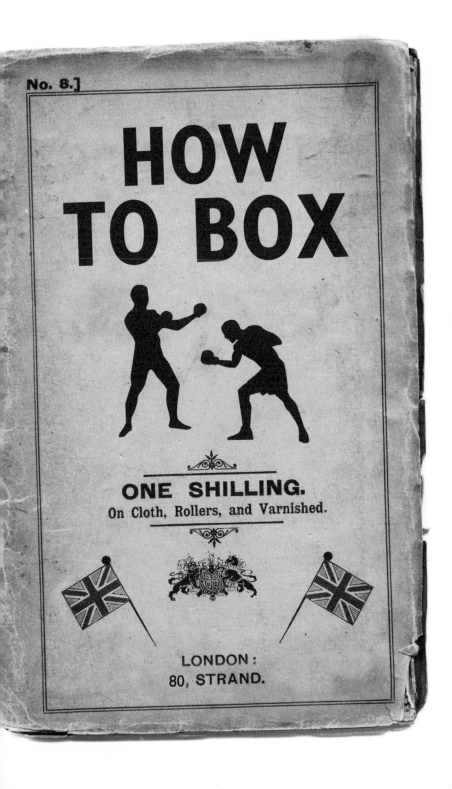

oxing is a sport where two opponents fight each other with their fists. A boxing match usually takes place in a specially designed ring and is supervised by a referee, with fighting taking place in short bursts called *rounds*. If a boxer is knocked down and cannot stand up before the referee counts to ten, the result is a knockout and the other fighter wins. If there is no knockout, the result is decided by judges using a scoring system.

Boxing opponents are matched in terms of weight. At the lighter end of the scale, terms are used such as *flyweight* and *bantamweight*, going up to the heavier *middleweight* and *heavyweight*.

There are seventeen major weight classes in professional boxing that enable fighters to be evenly matched.

Boxing weight limits:

Heavyweight – over 91kg

Cruiserweight – 91kg

Light heavyweight – 79kg

Super middleweight – 76.2kg

Middleweight – 72.5kg

Light middleweight (super welter) – 70kg

Welterweight – 66.7kg

Light welterweight (super light) – 63.5kg

Lightweight – 61.2kg

Super featherweight (junior light) – 59kg

Featherweight – 57.1kg

Super bantamweight (junior feather) – 55.3kg

Bantamweight – 53.5kg

Super flyweight (junior bantam) – 52.1kg

Flyweight – 51kg

Light flyweight – 49kg

Strawweight (mini fly or minimum) – 47.6kg

A good boxer needs to combine technical skill, speed, grace and aggression with many months of training. Boxers must learn how to attack and defend with a wide repertoire of punches, moves and counter-moves, all combined with skilful footwork.

There are four basic punches in boxing: the jab, the cross, the hook and the uppercut. These can be used in combination. Most boxers will try to use short, fast combinations and then will quickly move position to get out of their opponent's way.

Rapid movement is crucial to boxing as it helps avoid punches. There are several manoeuvres a boxer can use in order to evade or block a punch. Among them are bobbing and weaving, blocking, clinching and slipping.

Most boxers will try to get or keep to the centre of the ring in order to corner their opponent.

Biting, headbutting and hitting below the belt are not allowed.

Boxing – A Short History: Part Two

In modern boxing the first version of the rules we use today were introduced in 1743 by the man who is now known as the father of English boxing: legendary London champion Jack Broughton. He devised them as a measure to protect boxers, who sometimes died in the ring. Among the new rules it was stated that two umpires should be present to prevent disputes and no man should be hit when he is down.

Bare-knuckle boxing is when two individuals fight each other without boxing gloves; it is the original form of boxing. Bare-knuckle boxing became popular in England during the early eighteenth century in the form of contests known as prizefighting. Kicking, gouging, grappling, biting, headbutting and hitting below the belt were all allowed ... because there were no referees and no rules. However, in many ways, bare-knuckle boxing is less dangerous than standard boxing because boxing gloves make it possible to punch a rival very hard without smashing the bones in the punching hand.

Location: Austria

James travels by ferry and train from Dover to Kitzbühel in Austria to meet up with Mr Merriot's school group for the Easter break. The school skiing trip is a challenging experience and James is lucky to survive it. Months later, James finds himself returning to Austria under very different circumstances.

Located in south-central Europe, Austria is landlocked and shares borders with eight other countries. Dominated by the Alps in the western, southern and central regions, much of its landscape is mountainous with snowfields and glaciers. Other parts of the country are covered by forest and woodland. The Danube is its main river.

Capital city: Vienna Population: Approx. 8,300,000
Area: 83,872 km². Languages spoken: Mainly German
speaking, also Slovene, Croatian, Hungarian

Flag:

AUSTRIA — Short History

An emperor called Charlemagne conquered the region in 788, naming it Eastern March (which gives the country its modern-day name of Österreich). In 1278, the Hapsburgs gained power and this famous royal House went on to rule it for more than 600 years.

In 1867 Austria and Hungary were joined together, forming the large and powerful Austro-Hungarian Empire. The heir to the Austro-Hungarian throne, Archduke Ferdinand, was famously shot dead in 1914. This was the catalyst for the First World War (known at the time and shortly thereafter as the Great War), which caused utter devastation — and 16 million deaths — from 1914 to 1918. During the war, Austria–Hungary was one of the Central Powers allied to Germany, and who were eventually left humiliated and defeated.

In March 1938, German troops marched into Austria, and Adolf Hitler declared its union with Germany. A year later, the Second World War began and Austrian soldiers fought alongside German troops as part of the alliance called the Axis powers. They were eventually defeated in 1945.

Austria gained its independence in 1955 and became a member of the European Union in 1995.

SCALE

0   40
ENGLISH MILES

GERMAN

Innsbruck

SWITZERLA

Mountains and Memories

The dramatic Alpine landscape of snow-capped mountains and plunging valleys is a stunning sight, as James realizes when he first arrives in Austria. It reminds him of his early childhood in Switzerland.

'It was breathtaking. James stood for a moment just taking it all in. The scenery was perfect, and perfectly untouched. He felt like God on the first day of creation looking out over his handiwork.'

Despite their beauty, James is well aware of the dangers that lie in the mountains. His own parents died in this very same mountain range, in the western Alps in France.

THE ALPS

The Alps are Europe's dominant range of mountains, spanning from the Mediterranean coast of France, via Switzerland, Northern Italy and Austria, to Slovenia. The Alps cover much of Austria and the highest peaks rise to more than 3,700 metres. Austria's very highest peak is the 3,797-metre-high Mount Grossglockner.

The School Ski Trip

James and the rest of his Eton group are staying in the pretty medieval town of Kitzbühel, 762 metres up in the mountains. In the background lies the Kitzbühler Horn and the peak of the Hahnenkamm mountain, which is linked to the town by a cable-car.

James immediately takes a liking to his Austrian ski instructor, Hannes Oberhauser – a small, cheerful and fit-looking man who, surprisingly, walks with a limp. His uneven gait, however, is transformed the minute he puts on his skis.

'You should see him in action, a picture of grace and elegance. It's those few drops of Austrian waltzing blood in his veins, I think.'

Herr Oberhauser is an expert skier and a fine instructor. He spends the next few days teaching the boys the basics and notices that James is learning very fast.

'You have natural balance, you listen well and you seem to have no fear at all.'

Herr Oberhauser recommends Hannes Schneider's school at St Anton in the Arlberg to James, the place where he himself learnt to ski.

'St Anton has become the university of skiing, the Mecca for all those who love to ski.'

HANNES SCHNEIDER

Hannes Schneider is known as the father of modern skiing. As a ski instructor and guide at St Anton he developed a technique known as the 'Arlberg Method', which is still used today. It leads beginners from a simple snowplough to more difficult turns, like the parallel turn. Schneider's methods helped make skiing - once considered very dangerous - into a sport that millions of people now enjoy.

Hannes becomes a good friend to James. He makes it clear that James will always be welcome at his home if he ever returns to Austria.

A BEGINNER'S GUIDE TO SKIING

James is a complete beginner when he arrives in Kitzbühel. The first thing Herr Oberhauser teaches James is the 'snowplough', a simple move that slows you down, controls your movement and helps you to stop. It also forms the basis for many other turns.

'Make a V-shape with your skis, the tips almost touching, the back ends as wide apart as possible. Press the knees forward and keep your heels flat and the skis very slightly on their inner edges.'

Once you have mastered it and had some practice, you can start skiing, albeit slowly and clumsily. As James soon finds out, falling over (sixteen times in ten minutes) is part of the learning process.

On steep slopes the snowplough will slow you down but it won't stop you completely. You will need to turn your skis to one side so that they are both across the slope and not facing down it.

As James soon learns, one of the most important things to remember is to lean forward so that your body is at least at a right angle to the slope. This is called vorlage.

Most ski resorts have trails or 'runs', which are designed for different levels of skiers. These are usually marked green for beginners, blue for intermediates and black for advanced skiers.

James is pretty confident on his skis by the time his group ventures up the Hahnenkamm to try some faster runs.

SKIING THEN AND NOW

The oldest ski — little more than a wooden plank — was found in Sweden and proved to be over 4,500 years old. It was probably used by a hunter.

James learns to ski in the 1930s using equipment that looks quite different to that used today. His long skis are made of hickory wood edged with steel (a new development at the time) and his ski boots are really just leather lace-up hiking boots. There were no quick-release bindings or retaining clips, so he would still have been attached to his skis if he fell.

A modern-day skier would find it tricky to perform smooth turns and manoeuvres on James's somewhat clunky apparatus. Over the years, ski equipment has become ever more sophisticated, helping skiers to perform better and faster on challenging terrain. Modern skis are now made from wood laminates, carbon fibre and a man-made substance called Kevlar, making them lightweight and more effective. They are also easier to control and make turns with, especially on steep slopes.

During this challenging run, a heavy fog descends, and Miles Langton-Herring and James become separated from the rest of their group. After an uncomfortable night in a mountain rescue hut, James is forced to pull the now-injured Miles down the mountain by sledge. Unfortunately, they dislodge a sheet of loose snow and are quickly caught up in one of the most dangerous events that can occur in a mountain environment – an avalanche.

'Slowly his senses returned and he felt a great weight pressing in on him from all sides, as if he was gripped in a huge fist. He couldn't move at all. It was then that he panicked and tried to shout for help, only to find that his mouth was blocked. He shook his head and struggled to spit and felt something cold and rough pressing against his face.

It was snow. He had been buried alive by the stuff.'

James is terrified and has to control his panic. The weight of the snow pressing on his chest makes it difficult to breathe and even the tiniest effort to move costs a huge amount of energy.

'Then an awful thought struck him – he had no idea which way was up and which was down. He could be lying on his front for all he knew, or even upside-down.'

SURVIVING AN
AVALANCHE

Avalanches claim 150 lives worldwide every year. Most victims are people enjoying mountain sports, such as skiers, snowmobilers and climbers, particularly those who venture 'off piste' or into unknown terrain.

An avalanche is clearly easiest to survive when avoided altogether. Before venturing out on a mountain trip, use local information and find out the weather forecast, areas to be avoided and any possible avalanche warnings. Safety equipment can also be taken – a snow beacon will beep to show rescuers your location if you are buried in the snow (though it does not have a huge range). Avalanche cords are long lightweight red cords that attach to the belt and drag behind you. In an avalanche the cord should stay on top of the snow, showing your location.

All avalanches need a trigger to set them off and there are lots of factors, among them temperature, slope angle, wind direction and the condition of the snow. Many avalanches are triggered by the people that end up trapped in them.

Avoiding dangerous areas

Look at the terrain for signs of obvious avalanche paths where vegetation is missing or damaged. If an avalanche has occurred before, it is likely to happen again.

1. If you have to travel on a potentially risky slope, always move in straight lines upwards or downwards – never traverse back and forth as this is more likely to set off movement. Try to travel only one person at a time.

2. Use any wooded areas, ridges or rocky outcrops as safe houses. Spend as little time as possible on the open slopes.

How to survive an avalanche

If the worst happens and you are caught up in an avalanche, you will need to think fast. Statistics show that fully buried avalanche victims must usually be found and dug out within 15 minutes to have a reasonable chance of survival.

You hear a rumbling sound and look up to see a wall of snow heading straight for you. What do you do?

 Move to the side of the avalanche as fast as you can. You need to avoid the centre of the flow where the snow is moving the fastest.

 Get rid of your skis, poles or rucksacks as they will drag you down. If you do not have time to take off your skis, follow Miles Langton-Herring's advice:

'Get your hands to your boots and grip your ankles, that way you can undo your skis so that you are not trapped under the snow...'

Seek shelter behind trees or rocks. Grab hold of your tree and brace yourself for the impact. The snow may take you and the tree with it but you might not get buried so deeply.

Try to cover your nose and mouth, or at least keep your mouth firmly closed, during the avalanche. Do not shout or scream.

As the avalanche begins to slow:

Bring your hands and arms up to your face to create an air space. Just before the snow settles, take a deep breath, making your chest expand for a few seconds. This may give you some breathing space when the snow hardens.

Try to kick yourself to the surface just before the snow comes to a complete stop. Don't try to 'swim' against the tide of the snow, do your best to move in the same direction.

James Bond: The Future

"'So, young James," he said.
"What is to be done with you?'"

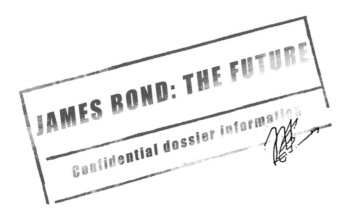

JAMES BOND: THE FUTURE

Confidential dossier information

By the time James comes to the end of his Austrian adventure, he is a changed person. He has seen and experienced a great deal, perhaps too much for a young boy. And he has come to realize that the world is a complicated place, a place where allegiances are complex and where people get caught up in shadowy conspiracies that are larger than they could ever imagine.

James's future hangs in the balance but he knows that this part of his life is over. No one must ever know the full truth about him, so it is decided that he will not return to Eton but instead attend Fettes boarding school in Scotland, where his father once went.

But James's life is just a small piece of a much bigger picture. Mr Merriot talks to him about what is happening in the world and how war might change everything.

'Hitler could become very troublesome. We know the Nazis will try anything to overrun Austria...'

THE APPROACH OF THE SECOND WORLD WAR

Throughout the 1930s extreme political movements, such as Fascism, grew and prospered against a background of political instability and economic crisis. Extremist leaders – Hitler in Germany, Mussolini in Italy, and Stalin, the leader of the Soviet Union – came to power and adopted aggressive foreign policies.

Adolf Hitler and his National Socialist party – known as the Nazis – gained popular support in Germany, and Hitler became Chancellor in 1933. Seeking to expand their territory, Hitler sent German troops into the Rhineland in 1936, then went on to occupy Austria in March 1938, declaring a union between the two countries. Despite talks and agreements with other countries, the Germans broke their promises and later seized all of Czechoslovakia. On 1 September 1939, Germany invaded Poland.

Britain and France declared war on Germany on 3 September.

The Second World War (1939–45) would go on to become the deadliest and most widespread conflict in history. By its end, approximately 55 million people were dead and the world was left in turmoil.

James does not know if, or how, he might one day be involved in this as-yet-unknown war, but for the moment he is content just to have some quiet time for reflection. The game is certainly not over and there will be plenty more challenges to come his way.

As Mr Merriot says:

'Perhaps our destinies are chosen for us.'

Acknowledgements

Every effort has been made to trace the copyright holders.
The publishers would like to hear from any copyright holder not acknowledged.

Images: p. 77 courtesy of the Popul Vuh Museum, City of Guatemala; pp. 90–1 map and p. 96 photo from *An Eton Camera, 1850–1919*, courtesy of Michael Russell Ltd; p. 122 courtesy of *mikes.railhistory.railfan.net*; p. 127 Keystone/Getty Images; p.156 Fox Photos/ Stringer/Getty Images; p. 157 Popperfoto/Getty Images; p. 144 courtesy German Federal Archive; p. 172 copyright © de Agostini Editore Picture Library; p. 175 courtesy of the Natural History Museum, London, copyright © Dorling Kindersley/Colin Keates; p. 184 copyright © Aston Martin Heritage Trust; p. 186 copyright © Wouter Melissen 2009; pp. 192–3 copyright © the *Daily Mail*; p. 202 copyright © Science Museum/SSPL; p. 203 David Crossland/Alamy; p. 215 copyright © Interfoto/Alamy; p. 217 copyright © Amazon-Images/Alamy; p. 220 copyright © Reuters/Corbis; p. 231 copyright © Dorling Kindersley/ Rough Guides.

Akenhead and Torquemada clues on p. 102 taken from *The Greatest Puzzles of All Time* by Matthew J. Costello, published by Dover Publications, copyright © Matthew J. Costello, 1996, used by permission of Dover Publications.